Florence
A MISSIONARY IN CHINA

———★———

M. J. PAULSON

M. J. Paulson Publishing
mjpaulson@abnorth.com

Copyright © 2018 by Marguerite Paulson
First Edition—January, 2019

All rights reserved
No part of this publication may be reproduced in any form, or by any means, electronic or mechanical, including photocopying, recording, or any information browsing, storage, or retrieval system without permission in writing from the publisher.

Cover and Interior Design by Donna Antkowiak
Cover art of China map: Designed by Freepik
Editing by Andrew Wilmot

ISBN
978-1-9994927-0-0 (Paperback)

1. BIOGRAPHY & AUTOBIOGRAPHY
2. RELIGION/Christian Living/Personal Memoirs

Distributed to the trade by the Ingram Book Company
Printed in the USA

Table of Contents

Death of Florence 1

Biography of Florence 3

Departure for China 7

China in the 1930s 13

Language School at Hwaining 19

Language School Routine 25

Posting to Kweiki 29

Kuling 33

Kweiki 37

Hokow 39

Letters from Hokow 47

War with Japan 53

Shanghai 59

Kiangtu 63

Chefoo 69

Shangjao 73

Mrs. Cheng 79

Chefoo Under Advisement 87

Yangkow 91

Chefoo Under Japanese Control 93

Doolittle Raid 111

Flight from Yangkow 121

Temple Hill 125

Kunming 131

Departure from Temple Hill 139
Weihsien 145
Eric Liddell 155
Tipton and Hummel 159
Liberation of Weihsien 165
Homeward Bound 169
Genealogy 175
Clifford Theodore Paulson 177
China Inland Mission 183
Chiang Kai-shek's Conversion to Christianity 185
Alfred Bosshardt and Arnolis Hayman 189
Boxer Uprising 195
John and Betty Stam 209

Bibliography 217
About the Author 221
Acknowledgements 223

Photographs

Florence with Elaine (cover picture)
Florence Annie Bradley 99
Florence and Clifford's wedding picture 99
Florence and Clifford's prayer card 100
Cliff, Florence, Philip, Kester, Kalbitz and Smail, Hill,
   Cronhielm and Carlson 100
Clifford, Philip and Mr. Bareis 101
CIM headquarters in Shanghai 101
Ascent to Kuling 102
Entrance into Kuling 102
Main street in Kuling 102
Florence with Philip 103
Philip 103
Philip and Chinese friends 103
Philip and Elaine 104
Philip, Clifford, Florence, Elaine and baby Keith 104
Florence, Clifford, Keith, Elaine and Philip 105
Keith 105
Elaine, Florence, Clifford, Blake and Keith in Canada 106
Keith, Elaine, Philip, Blake, Clifford, Florence, Duane, Lucille,
   Marguerite 1952 106
Marguerite and Florence, Peking 107

Maps

Map of Chinese Provinces 108
Map of China 1930 109
Map of Japanese Occupation 110

Diagrams

Language School Compound 23
Weihsien Concentration Camp 144

v

To those who have gone before,
And
To those who have come after,
In honour of Him!

I

Death of Florence

July 11, 2007

Florence, at ninety-nine years of age, died in an extended care room in a small community hospital in northern Alberta, her youngest daughter and a friend by her side. A small blue CD player, placed by her right ear, was playing "What a Friend We Have in Jesus." Clifford, her husband of fifty-five years, had died in 1986.

After her death, a booklet titled *Great Hymns and Their Stories* was found amongst her "important papers." The first song in the booklet was "What a Friend We Have in Jesus."[1]

Are we weak and heavy laden,
Cumbered with a load of care?
Precious Saviour, still our refuge,
Take it to the Lord in prayer.

Do thy friends despise, forsake Thee?
Take it to the Lord in prayer.
In His arms He'll take and shield Thee,
Thou wilt find a solace there.

---

[1] Joseph Scriven wrote a poem that formed the basis for this hymn to comfort his ailing mother. It was never intended for any eyes but hers. He told a neighbour, "The Lord and I did it between us." He himself had suffered incredible grief in his younger years when the lady to whom he was engaged accidentally drowned the day before their wedding.

II

Biography of Florence

In all thy ways acknowledge Him, and He shall direct thy paths.
(Proverbs 3:6)[2]

Florence Annie Bradley was born in the small town of Olds in central Alberta on June 18, 1908. Her parents, Edwin and Ada Bradley, along with their oldest daughter, Frances, had emigrated from England to Canada some time earlier. Several years later the family moved to Stettler.

When Florence was three years old, her father died. After over-exerting himself digging a deep well by hand and then going to his job as a switch operator for the railway, he died suddenly of heart failure. To support her four children, Florence's mother Ada took in washing. When the washing was done, Florence and her younger brother, Ted, would haul the huge bundles of laundry across town for delivery. They were paid five cents for their help. Her two older sisters, Frances and Gladys, helped with the family's finances by cleaning people's houses.

Florence's mother was a rather unique, independent woman. She would put on her hat whenever she answered the door to their small house. If it was someone she did not really feel like seeing, she would say, "Oh, I'm so sorry. I was just going out." But, if it happened to be someone she really wanted to see, she would then say, "Oh, what a pleasant surprise. I just got home."

Ada and her children attended the Anglican Church. When the church offered a prize for whoever could memorize a set number of Bible verses, Florence proudly recited all of them. But when she went to claim her prize, she was refused, with the disclaimer that the contest was meant for adults, not children. Florence was deeply offended at a promise not kept. Thereafter, or

---

[2] A Bible verse often quoted by Florence.

maybe even before, any promises she made were always fulfilled, no matter the cost or inconvenience to her. And while at times she regretted certain promises, she would still follow through, and be mindful of her words in the future.

Ada was a firm believer in education, and all her children were expected to have a vocation. Florence wanted to be a teacher and subsequently trained at the Teachers Training College in Camrose, where she first met her future husband, Clifford. After graduating, she taught at various schools in the area, travelling to them each day by horseback.

Florence always rode bareback, being unable to afford a saddle. After a full day of teaching in a one-room school, she would return to the farm house where she boarded, and water, feed, and bed her horse. She would go on to have supper with the family of the house, and then, in winter temperatures that dropped to minus thirty degrees, proceeded to crawl under thick blankets to try and keep warm in the unheated premises.

While visiting her sister Frances in Calgary, Florence ran into Clifford again. Although Florence had been saved in her younger years, Clifford was not a Christian. One Sunday night while walking by the First Baptist Church in southwest Calgary, he heard the singing and walked in to listen to the service. At the close of the evening, he went forward in answer to the altar call. Now, with his new-found faith and the same commitment as Florence to spiritual matters, the couple started going together and, on February 7, 1931, they were married.

Early in their married life, Florence and Clifford heard the call of the Lord to China. Clifford had been asked to start a Bible College in northern Alberta, at Sexsmith. He refused, however, stating, "No, I want to try the door of China first."[3]

In 1931, the couple attended Prairie Bible Institute (PBI) at Three Hills, Alberta in preparation for the ministry. Founded by a small group of farmers in 1922, one of PBI's primary purposes was to instil in their students knowledge of the word of God. Their motto was: "To Know Christ and Make Him Known." On October 29, 1933, a number of months after graduation, the couple's first child, Philip Timothy, was born.

---

[3] Thiessen, p. 72.

Florence: A Missionary in China

Florence's belief in God stemmed from an early age. In November 1934, her testimony was printed in the China Inland Mission's monthly periodical, *China's Millions.*

> In the quiet of my bedroom, after a Wednesday night prayer meeting in the town of Stettler, Alberta, I gave my heart to the Lord. Looking back on the years which have just passed, I am filled with gratitude to my Lord for His patience and loving-kindness in dealing with me. One day, while teaching in a little country school, I received from someone a tract which was a great blessing to me. This tract stressed doing all things as unto God, and it stated simply that a mountain flower bloomed as sweetly, and gave off the same delightful perfume, where no eye but God could see, as one that bloomed by the roadside, where many beheld its beauty. The following year a missionary address by Kenneth Grubb of Africa awakened in me a deep sense of my responsibility to the unevangelized of the world.
>
> About three and a half years ago, a month after my marriage to Mr. Paulson, I attended a Bible conference at Three Hills, where my soul was greatly blessed and where I fully surrendered my life to God. It was after this conference that we made our decision to go into active service. The Lord graciously met my every need with a promise from His Word. When I was doubtful, Psalm 37:5 guided me aright; when I was persecuted, Matthew 5:11, 12 consoled me; and when I found it hard to give up the comforts of this life, Mark 10:29, 30 gave me joy in putting my all upon the alter.
>
> After graduating from the Prairie Bible Institute, we spent a year in pastoral work under the Christian and Missionary Alliance in central Alberta, and now He is sending me to dark China with that precious promise, "Ye shall go out with joy, and be led forth with peace" (Isaiah 55:12).

Florence's personality suited her well for the mission field. She was tenacious, intrepid, adventuresome, and stoical. She played ice hockey in her adolescent years and was a strong competitor. Most importantly, however, she was unwavering in her belief in God and held strong values. If undercharged at a store she would walk back in and return the few pennies owing; if she was overcharged, she would go back to collect her change.

A sense of fear never marred her life. Whether an attribute of fearlessness or an unfailing belief in God's protection, she believed in the God who said,

> Fear thou not; for I am with thee: be not dismayed; for I am thy God: I will strengthen thee; yea, I will help thee; yea, I will uphold thee with the right hand of my righteousness. (Isaiah 41:10)

Years later, having grown old, she returned to China. In Shanghai, a taxi was hired to take her for a drive in the countryside. When she was ready to return to the city, the taxi driver refused to take her back unless she paid him considerably more money. In fluent Chinese, this elderly white woman told the driver that he was a disgrace to his people and his heritage, and that she expected him to drive her back to Shanghai at the price that was originally quoted, which he promptly did. Another time, Florence and her youngest child were walking at night down several streets filled with drunks holding bottles of beer and wine, prostitutes and their pimps, and people gambling on sidewalks with dice. Her small child did not remember where they'd come from or where they were going, just that it was a long way from home. Florence showed no signs of uneasiness or fear; neither did the child, for any fear from an adult produces the very same in a child.

Florence was very demonstrative and affectionate as a young girl, but, after being laughed at for her open displays of emotions, she learned to keep them to herself. Her stoicism is evident in her letters home from the mission field. Despite the dangers and difficulties of the times, she saw little need to detail them. God was in control and that was all that mattered.

Probably the most fitting description of Florence came late in life, when her husband, Clifford, who was by then in a nursing facility in Calgary, saw her walking down the hallway and asked, "Who is that woman?" When he was told, "That is your wife, Florence," he replied, "She is a good woman."

III

Departure for China

It may not be on the mountain height,
Or over the stormy sea,
It may not be at the battle's front
My Lord will have need of me;

But if, by a still, small voice He calls
To paths that I do not know,
I'll answer, dear Lord, with my hands in Thine.
I'll go where you want me to go.

I'll go where you want me to go, dear Lord,
Over mountain, or plain, or sea;
I'll say what you want me to say, dear Lord;
I'll be what you want me to be.[4]

In September of 1934, Florence, her husband, Clifford,[5] and their 10-month-old son, Philip, set sail for China. Florence was 26 years old. She left behind the only country she had ever known, her widowed mother and the rest of her family. Both she and Clifford felt called to China as missionaries and now they were finally going.

The young family set sail on September 15, 1934 from Los Angeles, travelling on a Norwegian freight ship across the Pacific. Florence wrote to her sister from the boat:

---

[4] "I'll Go Where You Want Me To Go," a hymn written by Mary Brown.
[5] Appendix B.

M. J. Paulson

Klaveness Line
Pacific Coast Asiatic Service

On Board M.S. Corneville
October 6th, 1934

Dear Frances,

We will soon be to the Yellow Sea now. We saw land for the first time yesterday since leaving Los Angeles 13 days before. The island was uninhabited, a large mass of rock like a small mountain. The coloring was beautiful. We have had most delightful weather for travelling. The Southern route which we travel is very warm. A person can be on deck all day and in the evening with a voile dress on. The men have their shirt sleeves rolled up, collars open and some wear white trousers. There are eight of us in our party, Rev. Mr. Kalbitz from St. Louis, Rev. Mr. Kester from Los Angeles, Mr. Roland Hill from Halifax, James Smail from Sioux St. Marie, Mr. Carlson from Prince George B.C. and Count Ulf Cronhielm from Sweden, recently from Toronto. Mr. Hill is a very fine singer and Mr. Kester is our best preacher. We have services every Sunday on the boat, the boys taking turns preaching or conducting the Bible class.

The crew, outside the officers which are Norwegian, are all Chinese most of who wear native dress. We have a very fine Captain who has a little dog named Topsy. Topsy got her tail cut off so now she has a rag on the stump of it. The cargo consists of 3,000,000 bd. ft. of lumber, 57 cows, 1 horse, 3,000 barrels of oil, 1400 tons of coal oil. The horse goes to the Sultan of some state near Hong Kong.

Philip has grown considerable since we left Vancouver. He took a few steps alone. He walks and runs by just taking one hand. He waves his hand and says bye bye. He likes the Chinese boys and wants to go to them whenever he sees them. His hair is all ringlets from the dampness. It is so damp that everything metal rusts even to the corners of trunks. We have just finished afternoon tea and the sea getting rough I didn't feel like finishing this letter.

I went up on deck where we could see sharks swimming around. They are a beautiful blue color but one shudders when they think of anyone getting into their clutches. When we watched them we little knew what kind of night we would spend at sea. The wind was blowing against the current so that great waves broke over the ship filling the deck with a few feet of water. We had to close our port holes and stay down in our cabins. During the night we continually heard a bang as a great wave broke over the ship. The boat was stopped as we drifted out in the Pacific. At five o'clock there was a terrible bang and the ship shivered then a plunge sideways till the water came over the side, just then a flash and fire and smoke in our cabin. The electric light fuse blew out and we were left in the dark. Philip began to cry so I had to quieten him while Cliff crawled out of his drenched bed. It was wonderful how the Lord gave us peace and quiet through it all while the sharks swam round to devour us. The ship was sturdy and so no damage was done. The sea was rough all day yesterday and hasn't calmed down much to-day. We expect to be in Shanghai to-morrow afternoon so to-day we expect to be busy getting ready. Philip is having his morning nap so we will have to do our packing this afternoon.

On October 15, 1934, after a month at sea, the family docked in Shanghai. At last they were in China, a country of 450 million people and four million square miles of land. A new dawn was rising.

Sailing into Shanghai, they noticed that the waters were filled with fishing boats and sampans—small flat-bottomed skiffs on which people lived and traversed the waterways of China. All cooking, washing and sleeping were done on board, with only a tiny little cover over part of the skiff for protection. Washing was hung on lines strung across the front of the sampan or hung on long bamboo poles sticking out from the end. Typically the boats were propelled by long poles but could also be propelled by sails, towed behind another larger vessel or hauled by ropes from the shore.

Shanghai, at that time, was a major seaport and commercial centre situated in Kiangsu Province on the east coast of China. Three million souls lived there. As ships pulled into the harbour, tall elegant buildings seemed to rise out of the water. The World Book of 1923 described Shanghai as two distinct communities. There was the old part of Shanghai with its narrow, open sewaged streets and typical Chinese houses and shops, surrounded by an ancient wall stretching for several miles along the left bank of the Huang-pu River.

Adjoining the old section of the city on the north and extending along the river for about three-fifths of a mile was commercial Shanghai. Commercial Shanghai was very European in appearance. It covered 5,362 acres and had broad, paved, well-lit streets, an efficient sanitary system, hospitals, schools and other modern structures. There were great walled estates, home to diplomats and businessmen, expensive hotels, banks and other businesses. Some of the buildings had actually been transported from Paris and London and reassembled in Shanghai. A fine esplanade, or Bund, skirted the river bank opposite an attractive park. The city contained warehouses, shipyards, cotton, silk, flour and paper mills, packing houses and other manufacturing establishments. It was a city controlled by European investment and management, and home to a substantial number of foreigners under the civil, criminal and political jurisdiction of their own consuls.

At Shanghai, the Paulsons and their baggage went through the chaos of customs and immigration. They were met by staff of the China Inland Mission (CIM)[6] under whom they were deployed. The Mission compound was situated in the International Settlement, which housed most of the foreigners in Shanghai. The compound was gated, with green lawns and flowers, and contained a large six storied building of light coloured stone and stucco. Balconies with iron rails edged each suite of rooms and arched windows decorated the top floor which housed a small but well-equipped hospital for Mission staff and missionaries. This was the hospital where Florence's next two children would be born.

Florence continued her letter to her sister.

We have now been in Shanghai five days. Mr. Slade & Mr. Griffin met us. Mr. Griffin brought me to the Home while Cliff & others looked after the luggage. The Home is very large. The weather is like August in Alberta. The nights are warm too. Philip has a cold just now. We all have to wear hats lined with red or helmets as the sun here is treacherous even when it is not shining on dull days. I had a Chinese hat made. It is a soft blue stitched with large brim in blue color. I like it very much. I also had a wadded gown made and two cotton slip-over gowns. The hat and gowns cost $22.50 mex[7] or about $7.75 gold. We had to get mosquito nets to have over the beds. I had a silk helmet given me and Cliff bought one for $4.00. Philip had a pair of knitted rompers, 3 knitted suits 2 blue & one white, 2 caps, scarf, 3 pair socks, sound leggings, woollen blanket given him by "Helping Hands" in England.

Shanghai is a very interesting city. The shops have no windows but open right out on the streets and have doors like garage doors on at night. As you go up the street the Chinese are making wadded quilts, cooking food, changing

---

[6] Appendix C.
[7] Mexican silver dollars. In 1934, one Mexican dollar was worth 38 cents in U.S. money.

money, etc. This morning on the way to church we saw the gaily decorated chair of a bride-to-be but we did not have time to stay & see the bride. The men with the rickshaws are everywhere seeking passengers. We had a ride Tues. night and it was great fun. The people are lovely and we are enjoying it.

Cliff has to preach to-night in the Free Christian Church.

We expect to leave to-morrow for Hwaining. I will close for this time.

Yours with much love,
Florence, Cliff, Philip

IV
China in the 1930s

The horse is prepared against the day of battle: but safety is of the Lord. (Proverbs 21:31)[8]

In 1934, the China that Florence and Cliff encountered was riddled with political unrest, war, disease, and death. The times were certainly troubled and troubling. China was just beginning to emerge from an old feudal system, and various factions were vying for control.

In 1911, revolutionaries overthrew the Manchu Dynasty, which had ruled China since 1644, and China was declared a Republic with Dr. Sun Yat-Sen as the first president. During the turmoil of the revolution, various parts of China were taken over by Manchurian or bandit leaders who became known as warlords. Each had their own sovereign rule and militia. Although Dr. Sun was president of a few territories in southern China, his goal was to unite all of China under one central government, and his party, the Kuomintang, worked toward that end. The government later included the Communist Party, which had been formed in China in 1920 and was supported by Russia. It too wanted a unified China with one central government, but under Communist rule.

In 1925, Sun Yat-Sen died of liver cancer and Chiang Kai-shek, a military leader who would later become a Christian,[9] assumed control of the government. Like Dr. Sun, Chiang wanted to bring the remaining territories, which were still under control of the warlords, together to form one China. In 1927, as commander of the Chinese Nationalist Army, Chiang violently purged the government of Communists; this action plunged China into a twenty-two-year civil war. Blood was being spilled everywhere in China, between the Nationalist and Communist armies, and the guerrillas and the

---
[8] A Bible verse extensively quoted by Cliff in prayer when traveling.
[9] Appendix D.

warlords. But the peasants, caught in the crossfire, suffered the most, and there were casualties amongst Westerners and missionaries as well.

By this time, Mao Tse-tung was one of the major leaders of the Communist forces, which were heavily concentrated in Hunan and Kiangsi, where Florence and Cliff were later to be stationed. From 1931 to 1933, heavy fighting was taking place in Kiangsi between Nationalist and Communist forces. In October 1934, after major defeats, the Communist leaders called for the remaining remnants of their forces to come together and reorganize in northwest China. This retreat, which occurred between 1934 and 1936, became known as "The Long March." Five CIM missionaries—Alfred and Rose Bosshardt, Arnolis and Rhoda Hayman and their two children, and Grace Emblen—were taken captive along the way,[10] although the wives and children were released shortly thereafter. Later, Grace was able to make her escape when she lagged behind during the march.

Continual warfare was not the only peril Florence and Clifford faced. Alongside the rising tide of nationalism sweeping China were anti-foreign sentiments and resentment. Reaction to the Imperialism of the West was intense. For not only had the Western Powers imposed unequal treaties on China in the past, they had stripped it of its silver and plundered its natural resources in exchange for opium, which they had forced on China as a commodity of trade. They also controlled China's customs and engaged in extraterritoriality, which protected their own citizens from prosecution if they committed a crime in China. Demonstrations against any form of foreign domination of Chinese life were common. The most notable expression of anti-foreign hostilities occurred in 1900, when the Boxers[11] besieged the foreign community in Peking and murdered a large number of missionaries, their Christian converts, and other foreigners in the province of Shansi and surrounding territories. Later, in 1927, anti-foreign riots were so violent that all foreigners in the interior of China were forced to exit to the coast. Then, in the early 1930s, with similar activity in Nanking, which was now the capital of China, all foreigners were advised to leave the city. For the most part, however, the unrest was primarily in the coastal or major cities, where most

---

[10] Appendix E.
[11] Appendix F.

of the foreigners and missionary societies had settled, and less in the rural areas.

The Mission's expectations during these and other times were "that missionaries would share in the trials that all of China was experiencing, that they would experience divine protection in the midst of those trials, and that if and when it was God's will and time, they would lay down their lives for the cause of Christ." (Roberts, p. 83)

Besides the danger from politicized forces, the countryside was full of roving bandits, and missionaries were prey to be robbed, beaten, or even killed whenever or wherever they travelled. As Alfred Bosshardt described, "If soldiers were not fighting in the vicinity, bandits were plundering. A journey of two or three days in the interior meant trouble. Communications were difficult, proper roads non-existent for thousands of miles. There were no hospitals or doctors within easy reach. Foreigners excited curiosity." (p. 35)

Then there was the filth of China and myriad diseases, including typhus, cholera, diphtheria, typhoid, scarlet fever, smallpox, tuberculosis, and the plague. There was also malaria, with its bone-racking chills and fevers, which Florence contracted and which periodically ravaged her body for the rest of her life. Having no immunity, foreigners were particularly susceptible to these illnesses, which continually decimated their numbers. Neel Roberts, in his account of CIM missionary efforts in China, noted that "with over a thousand workers on the field there were few months when there was no report of the death of a missionary or the need to send one home due to an untreatable disease." (p. 81)

Western sanitation did not exist in the China of the 1930s. Gutters, which ran alongside the streets in every city, town, and village, were used for waste water and as urinals, and it was not unusual to see babies being held over them or adults squatting there. Men urinated on the sides of buildings, and young children, with their wadded trousers slit underneath, squatted on the street to defecate. The faint odour of urine was ever present.

Human waste, called "night soil," was used to fertilize the crops and gardens. Fruits, vegetables, chickens, and hunks of meat were sold on the street in open stalls surrounded by flies and other insects, and their droppings. Fruit had to be disinfected. Pigs were often kept in large pits that were used as a human latrine and for other waste. Tea was the staple drink as all water had to be boiled.

Chinese kitchens were seldom cleaned and contained every bit of accumulated grime from the day they were first set up. The same pots were used over and over again for whatever was being cooked, and food was served in a communal bowl into which everyone dipped their already-used chopsticks.

Chinese houses had no glass in the windows, only coverings of sheets of rice paper or vegetable fibre,[12] and were terribly cold in winter and stifling hot in the summer. Frequent droughts and floods destroyed crops, and famines affected what food was available to eat.

If all these perils alone were not enough, there was also the threat of Japan closing in on China's back door. Imperialist Japan, in its ever-widening search for raw materials, had its eye on Manchuria in northern China, for its natural riches and industrial resources. In 1931, Japan annexed Manchuria, and over the next two years added the northern provinces of Chahar, Jehol, and eastern Hopei to its holdings. In the ensuing months, the Japanese army continued to move southward, mainly undeterred, as Chiang Kai-shek was singularly focused on eradicating the Communists. Only later, when Chiang Kai-shek realized that war with Japan was inevitable, and after being kidnapped by a Manchurian warlord who held to the Communist slogan that "Chinese must not fight Chinese," did he actually ally himself with the Communists to fight Japan.

Although Mao Tse-tung had always claimed that he wanted to fight Japan, and had utilized that claim to rally the peasants to the Communist movement, the Communist forces did not fight the Japanese to any great extent. By the Communists' own account, by 1939 their losses amounted to only 3 percent of all casualties, compared to the Nationalists' 97 percent.[13] In reality, the Communists' main objective was to enlarge their own territory, to propagandize amongst the Nationalist troops as a means of increasing defections and their own numbers, and to keep their own armies as intact as possible.[14]

---

[12] Vegetable fibre was quite durable as a windowpane. It was also very healthy in that it allowed soft light and ultraviolet rays to filter through the fibre.

[13] *The Generalissimo*, p. 169.

[14] *Red Star Over China*, p. 351.

Even when Communist troops were ordered to join Nationalist troops in a "united front," the Communist leaders would order their forces to move slowly—only "50 li each day, and pause one day after every three days."[15] There were also instances of Communist armies surreptitiously attacking government forces. All of these manoeuverings merged with the larger conflict of World War II.

This then was the China Florence and Clifford entered. First, however, they needed to learn the language and become acquainted with Chinese customs and ways.

---

[15] *The Generalissimo*, p. 147.

V

Language School at Hwaining

> . . . thou hast left thy father and thy mother, and the land of thy nativity and art come unto a people thou knowest not theretofore. The Lord recompense thy work and a full reward be given thee of the Lord God of Israel under whose wings thou art come to trust. (Ruth 2:11–12)

From Shanghai, Florence and her family travelled three hundred miles west by steamer along the Yangtze River to Hwaining, located in the southeast part of Anhwei Province. One of the oldest cities in China, Hwaining was founded during the Han dynasty in 200 B.C. The city was surrounded by high walls several feet thick, as well as a wooden gate, a moat, and a drawbridge. As a port city, it faced the Yangtze River on the south. To the north was an elongated low mountain called Longshan Mountain, to the west the Wanhe River, and to the east the Shitang and Pozhi lakes.

As the steamboat approached Hwaining, a smaller boat came out from shore and travelled alongside it. Passengers and baggage were transferred without either boat stopping. Once everything was unloaded, the small boat proceeded to shore where the passengers alighted. From there, Florence, Clifford, and young Philip travelled to the language school where they were to study the Chinese culture and language before venturing on to their first posting. Hwaining was specifically chosen for language training as the dialect there was similar to the Chinese spoken throughout the rest of the country.

A term at language school usually lasted eight or nine months. The CIM expected their missionaries to be conversant in Chinese and acclimatized to the food and social customs of the people before working amongst them. The male missionaries were trained at the Hwaining language school while the female missionaries went to Yangchow, near Shanghai. However, because Florence was married, she attended school with her husband. She was the only female missionary candidate, and her son Philip was the only white child. The language school itself was a large walled compound comprising massive lawns, tennis and volleyball courts, a playground for children (which included swings and teeter-totters), a four-storey grey brick administration building containing the church, a five-storey building that housed the missionaries and had a hospital on the top floor, and various buildings for the Chinese workers.

Most of Florence's day was spent studying the language and looking after Philip. The official Chinese language, Mandarin, is a very difficult language to master. The spoken language is tonal with four tones for each word. As the tone varies, so does the meaning of the word. To illustrate, the word *mai* with a falling rising tone means to buy, whereas mai with a simple falling tone means to sell. Thus, when a new word is learned, the tones must also be learned. Florence had some problems learning the language as she was tone deaf.

Clifford, however, had fun with the language, saying, "to hang the flag from the flagpole," and then changing the tone of the word flag to say, "to hang your mother-in-law from the flagpole." Florence never said if she was amused or not.

In turn, written Mandarin consists of a number of characters each representing a different word. For example:

mai "to buy"

mai "to sell"

In Mandarin, there are approximately 60,000 characters. Each character has to be learned separately along with its pronunciation and meaning. The characters are written in columns, starting at the right and going from top to bottom.

Florence wrote to her sister from Hwaining in December of 1934.

Florence: A Missionary in China

China Inland Mission
Hwaining, Anhwei

December 17, 1934

Dear Frances,

We have just finished our evening study period so I will endeavor to get a letter written before retiring for the night. We were a little indisposed at times on our trip but not so much as to send us to bed. Philip was sick once. He loves everybody so he doesn't mind where he is. If you give him anything good to eat he'll be your friend for life. One of the German fellows, Herman Bareis, took Philip to his room and gave him a small piece of chocolate. Now Philip wants to go to Mr. Bareis whenever he sees him. He walks all over now. He is outside nearly all day with his Chinese nurse, so he looks well. He is very strong. He can carry a basket, the basketball or a 2 lb tin all over. He eats porridge & 2 or 3 jap oranges for breakfast, yolk of egg soup, sweet potatoes, carrots and toast for dinner, porridge and fruit for supper, besides a couple bottles of milk a day. They do not have cows here so we have carnation milk. We have a Chinese meal every Tuesday. Eight sit at a table, on which is placed 9 bowls containing spinach, fish, white vegetable, turnips, meat balls, Chinese dishes composed of mushrooms, eggs, meat, to-fu, bean sprouts, etc. It is all very good. We are each given a bowl of rice and a pair of chopsticks. We help ourselves to one or all of the dishes and eat it with the rice. I especially like the fish, which is cooked with brown sugar and vinegar and served with the framework of the head still on. After eating our fill we go into the next room where we have bananas, oranges, cookies and tea.

Help is very cheap here to what it is at home but it takes about half a dozen to do one ordinary person's work. We pay the woman who looks after Philip $8.00 mex a month, which is equal to less than $3.00 of our money. She boards herself, comes at 7 a.m., has 1½ hours off before noon and then stays until 5:30 p.m. The Chinese vary in their eating. Some eat two meals a day, others 3 or 4. They won't eat or drink anything cold, everything must be hot.

There are 34 of us here as students studying the language. We have three teachers, Mr. Chang, Lui and Yen. They don't speak English so we have to speak to them in Chinese, draw or motion to make them understand. Philip's nurse does not know a word of English so have some great times understanding each other. Wed. evening we have a meeting, when one gives a talk on the particular kind of Christian work they have been engaged in. Sat. night we have prayer meeting and one gives his testimony. Sunday we have a service in Chinese at a quarter to eleven and one at 7 p.m. in English. We do not understand a great deal yet. There are 60,000 characters in Chinese and when we realize that Shakespeare's was only 3000, look at the task of mastering Chinese. However an ordinary Chinese scholar's vocabulary is only 6000 words. We do not have to do it in our own strength for the Lord is with us and enables us to acquire sufficient to meet our needs.

The buildings here are real Chinese fashion, the rooms practically all opening into a central court of grass and trees. We have some bushes covered with red berries, which are very pretty this time of year. The large trees have all lost their leaves but the bushes are still green and flowers are blooming. Some winters they have snow but not always. The weather has been very warm but it was drizzly to-day. The atmosphere is always quite damp but usually there is an abundance of sunshine. We have four large windows in our large room then we have a small room for studying while Philip is asleep. We have no blinds here but just broadcloth curtains, orange colored. The walls are white washed over the plaster. The floors are rough painted boards. The furniture is all black and consists of wardrobe, 2 wash stands, bed, cot, two chairs, long & square table and two chests of drawers, one with shelves for books above it. A straw mat covers the floor in our room. Everything is plain but comfortable. We have the luxury of electric lights. The boys have bath houses but I have to use a wooden tub as the Chinese don't think it proper for ladies & men to use the same bath.

The church here is run entirely by the Chinese themselves. You find all kinds like you do among the Christians at home. Some are content to attend on Sundays and others are out witnessing for the Lord Jesus Christ both in the city and away. Mr. Hsieh, one Christian here has been away seven years at a time preaching in practically every province in China. The cook here is a Christian and two kitchen boys but the other two servants are not.

I went to bed before I finished so now it is noon on Tuesday. The weather is still rainy. Philip is playing with the basketball. We have a basketball court, bean bag tennis and volley ball for exercise. Cliff is quite a player. The English beat the Americans 20:21 in an International game here at the school.

We didn't send any Christmas presents as they charge duty on things going out as well as in Canada, and a person is not always in a position to pay duty for presents. We can do no shopping for ourselves so we cannot very well get anything but real necessities. When we know the language we will be able to do some shopping. There are no foreign stores here so practically everything has to be sent from Shanghai.

I hope you all have a good Christmas but it will all be over before this reaches you.

May God keep you all in health and strength and increasing in the knowledge of our Lord Jesus Christ.

Love to all the family,
From Florence, Cliff & Philip

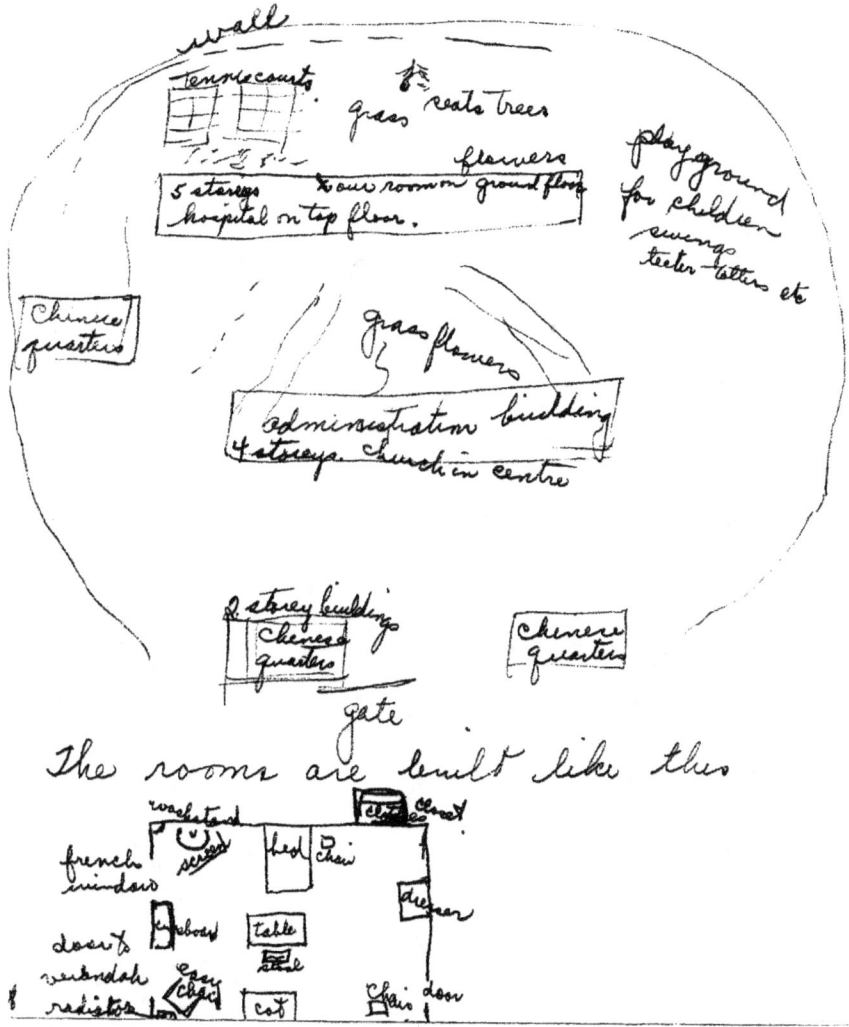

Language school compound at Hwaining and the Paulson's living quarters, 1934. Drawn by Florence

VI

Language School Routine

How then shall they call on him in whom they have not believed? and how shall they believe in him of whom they have not heard? and how shall they hear without a preacher?
And how shall they preach, except they be sent? as it is written, How beautiful are the feet of them that preach the gospel of peace, and bring glad tidings of good things! (Romans 10:14–15)

The schedule at Hwaining was hectic. Another missionary, Marion Springer, attending at a different time than the Paulsons, detailed the routine.

6:50 a.m.	Alarm goes off. We prepare for the day and have our morning prayers and Bible reading until
7:30 a.m.	Breakfast, after which we have morning devotions. The men take them in turn. We just finished John this morning, and tomorrow will be starting Acts. After this comes a time for odd jobs, such as refueling the stove, running errands, and reading the news.
9:00 a.m.	Starts our day of Chinese study. We have one group class where a Chinese teacher explains all the meanings of the words we are supposed to have had. It is very entertaining, for when he can't make us understand what he means by talking, he acts it out, and if that fails he draws a picture. To date, the most amusing was a Chinese version of Jonah. Also we have a class on grammar and an individual class with another Chinese teacher for pronunciation and tone. The rest of our study time we use in our rooms preparing for these classes.
12:00 M.	School is out for a while. Mail often comes at this hour, and of course we drop everything to read it.

12:30 p.m.	Dinner. Today we had Chinese food, eight bowls of various kinds of meat and vegetables in the middle of square tables, and bowls of rice at our places, with chopsticks. On Saturday we have another kind of Chinese food called "Mee-en", which is noodles cooked with shredded meat, bean-curd, and vegetables, and also is eaten with chopsticks.
1:45 p.m.	School begins again, for the afternoon session, to
4:00 p.m.	When we all turn out for outdoor exercise, basketball, volleyball, or deck tennis. If it is too rainy we play ping-pong. This ends in time so that everybody can get washed up for
5:30 p.m.	Supper. About this time the lights will go on. In most Chinese cities that have it, electricity is turned off during the day, but left on all night because Chinese like to sleep with a bright light to frighten away evil spirits. After supper we have prayer for the provinces, three a night, and of course for other things too.
7:00 p.m.	School again for one hour. Before this, a good many of us will be visiting or writing letters.
8:30 p.m.	On Wednesdays we have a meeting, where someone tells about some kind of life or work. Other days we have a time of prayer. All lights are supposed to be out at ten, and they nearly always are, for we all find we need much sleep.

On Saturdays we have a half-holiday, for games, baths, letters, and hikes. At night we have a prayer meeting, where one of the men tells how he came to be here, one of the high points of the week for us. Chinese church, Sunday morning, is Quaker-meeting style, with men on one side and women on the other. In our own little evening service the men take turns leading, and we pray for Sunday which is then just beginning in Europe. It is fine to feel it sweeping round the world, and worship and praise arising from every country. When we get up Monday morning it is Sunday afternoon in North America, and we pray for you all again, and just praise Him for giving us so many Christian friends!

When not studying, Florence and the others would often go for walks outside the city walls or visit various sites, one of which was the Zhenfeng Pagoda. The Pagoda was situated near a bend in the Yangtze River several miles from Hwaining. It was seven storeys high totaling 236 feet. Originally built in 1570 during the Ming Dynasty, it contained over 600 statues of Buddha. Each storey had a dozen or so niches for lanterns and it served as a lighthouse for ships at night.

Everywhere in the countryside were graves, small mounds of earth grouped together[16] or unburied coffins waiting for an appropriate day for the funeral. In the water-soaked rice fields, farmers using wooden implements pulled by water buffalo would be plowing, and women and children gathering straw to burn in their mud stoves. Closer to the city, other women would be washing their clothes in the river.

Florence wrote again to her sister in March of 1935.

China Inland Mission
Hwaining, Anhwei

March 17, 1935

Dear Frances,

Received your welcome letter. We are glad to know all are well. We have spent a very good winter. The weather now is delightful. The evenings and mornings are so nice and warm, any fire would make it too warm. It is raining to-day and it certainly knows how to pour steadily down. It takes no time for the big stone jars under the eaves to overflow. We have just come in from communion service. The text was Gal. 2:20. "I am crucified with Christ nevertheless I live yet not I but Christ liveth in me and the life I now live in the flesh I live by faith, in the Son of God who loved me and gave himself for me". When we realize the truth of that verse, that after we have experienced the new birth, that we have been crucified with Christ to all our own desires, worldly ambitions and that we are now to live unto God alone, who washed us and gave Himself for us, it is a new experience of power in our life. Although we are weak, full of faults and failings yet in Christ we have everything. All we have to do is to stretch out the arm of faith and take what Christ has already purchased for us. I didn't intend preaching a sermon when I sat down to write but these truths are worth pondering. God's word is true no matter what we may experientially feel.

We are nearing the end of our term here. In a month I do not know where we will be. We are very busy getting ready for our examination. We have to

---

[16] The Chinese put their dead on top of the ground and then pile dirt on top of the body.

read sections of the first chapter of Mark and John before Messrs Mair, Yen and Hu besides part of a reading lesson. The Lords prayer and 3 verses of Scripture we have to recite in Chinese. After living here nearly six months things Chinese are becoming a little more part of us. The names of places are becoming more familiar. We are able to understand a little of what is said and to learn a little about fellow members of the Mission. Mr. Gibb, the Mission Director, will be here the end of this month to designate us.[17]

Philip is quite a little man now. He understands pretty well all that is said to him but he is slow about talking. He gets along fine with all the young men, who make quite a pet out of him. They had him on the table trying to get him to conduct while they sang to him this afternoon. His special favorites are Mr. Bareis from Germany, and Mr. Conway from New Zealand. Everything he gets goes out the window or the door, buttons, facecloth, bottle of vise, his cup, papers or anything at all.

We have an apple, cherry and apricot tree in bloom in the yard. They did have an orange tree but it got frozen one year. The trees are just beginning to leaf out. Wild lilac and violets seem to be the only flowers out now except for the dandelion and a little blue climbing plant which is very pretty.

A couple young lady missionaries were at the Mission home for two weeks. They went back to their station on the bus yesterday. There are a few buses in this part of the country. We saw 9 aeroplanes fly over in a group one day last week. There are less than ten cars in the city. The streets are so narrow that for a car to go down it everyone would have to go into the shops there is hardly room for two rickshaws to pass. There are about 1000 rickshaws here in the city. We are never out of the compound except to go for a walk so we don't have any occasion to use one.

It is now Monday. We have spent another busy morning studying. We have half an hour between 12 and 12:30 before we have dinner. Philip has just awakened from his morning nap. He gets up at 6:15 a.m. so he sleeps from 10:30 to 12:00.

The sun is shining beautifully to-day. There are many birds singing around here. The Chinese keep big birds like meadow larks in a cage. Some of these birds can be taught to speak Chinese.

Yours with much love from all to all,
Florence, Cliff & Philip

---

[17] The CIM was hierarchically structured, headed by a General Director, then by Superintendents responsible for overseeing designated districts, and finally the missionaries, themselves.

VII

Posting to Kweiki

There never was a time when prayer on behalf of the work and workers in China, not to say the nation itself, was needed more than it is today.
(*China's Millions*, June 1935, p. 93)

In the late 1920s the province of Kiangsi was a hot bed of Communist activity, and Communist forces roamed the countryside bringing death and destruction with every footstep. Although considerable evangelistic work had been done in the province in the preceding thirty years, the Communists had spent their time eradicating all Christian endeavours, destroying the mission churches and persecuting the Chinese Christians. In Miriam Dunn's words, "Christians suffered cruelty and the churches stood empty." (p. 155)

Then came the civil war between the Nationalist government led by Chiang Kai-shek and the Communist Red Army. With increasingly decisive victories by the Nationalists, the Communists started to abandon the province, conscripting young Chinese men along the way. In the CIM's periodical, *China's Millions*, Rev. A. B. Lewis reported:

> The people . . . have suffered terribly under the Communists, and it is a rare thing to find a young man among them. When you do meet one, he is probably one who fled at the approach of the Reds and has now returned.
>
> Here is a sample of one of the tales of horror from this field. When the Communists had to flee . . . they called together the younger men of the peasants and people and asked which of them wanted to go with them and which of them wanted to stay where they were. Doubtless the number who really wanted to go with them were few, but some sensed possible danger and elected to go, the rest wished to stay. The Reds then ordered those who were ready to go to slay all those who had chosen to remain. (September 1935, p. 134)

Between the Communists and the Civil War, seven million people died in Kiangsi during this period of time. Hunan, which was also a Communist stronghold, suffered as well.

Following their military losses, the Communists commenced the Long March, proceeding from Kiangsi to northwest China, and the missionaries breathed easier. But their safety was not assured. John and Betty Stam,[18] a young CIM couple, were beheaded by the Communists on December 8, 1934, near Tsingteh in south Anhwei.

It was into this fray that Florence and Clifford silently marched. No fear or regret was ever expressed, only a desire to serve their Saviour.

By the spring of 1935, Florence and Clifford had completed their language training and were posted to Kweiki in Kiangsi Province. In May the family left for their posting stopping along the way at Kiukiang and Nanchang. Florence wrote her Mission newsletter, with a copy to her mother:

> If you were to follow the tramp, tramp of a number of feet up the stairway of the language school at Hwaining on the third of May, you would find yourself in a cozy room with eight other young people drinking a cup of coffee. Why this gathering? To-night we must part and be scattered to different parts of the great land of China, so the North American party have met for their last cup of coffee and word of prayer as a group. Just as we were about to begin word comes up, "The Paulsons must leave; telegram regarding the steamer has come". After a hurried "tsai huei" we gather together our last few belongings, dress Philip, and prepare for a rickshaw ride to a Chinese inn. Since the boat arrives early, it would mean travelling through the dark streets at three in the morning with many dogs snapping at your heels, so for Philip's sake we stayed in an inn at the water's edge.
>
> Have you ever been to a Chinese inn? Follow me into a small room overlooking a busy street. No blinds adorn the windows thus allowing those who pass by to gaze in, and the wooden slats remind you of a prison. Upon arriving, a Chinese brings a teapot of hot water and several bowls. Looking around the room, you see a hat rack, small dresser, and a bed. The bed has no mattress, only two quilts and a small, hard pillow. The walls were so thin that we could clearly hear the snores of those in the next room.

---

[18] Appendix G.

Florence: A Missionary in China

At 4 a.m. we were astir, and at 6:30 we boarded the big river steamer from a small boat as it slowed up in midstream. Miss McKenzie (an older worker) and two new lady workers for Kiangsi greeted us when we came on deck. The day was dull but we enjoyed our trip up the Yangtze, landing at Kiukiang at 5:30 at night. Mr. Kalbitz and Mr. Paulson had their eyes tested at the Water of Life hospital during the stay at Kiukiang. The following Monday, we all attended the King's Accession Celebration on board the British gunboat H.M.S. Scarab, after which a tasty little lunch was served.

On Wednesday, we took the train to Nanchang, it being our first train ride in China. The trains are much smaller than those of the homeland. The windows were very small. The third class cars had wooden benches and the second class had leather covered seats. Food was brought through the train at meal times and sold by young men in clean white suits. On the train we were able to speak to some of the Chinese in the English language and deal with them about the Lord. To the other passengers tracts were given. At Nanchang we were met by Mr. Glazier, and after a long ferry ride and rickshaw ride we finally arrived at the C.I.M. home. We also had the privilege of fellowship with Mr. & Mrs. Porteous at the Bible School in Nanchang. Mr. & Mrs. Porteous, you will remember, were in the hands of the Red bandits for a hundred days.

On the Friday, I had the pleasure of visiting the soldiers' hospital. The main building is one long ward with numerous small wards on each side. White iron cots with a wadded quilt and small stands are the only furniture. The soldiers were lying on the cots, but as we entered most of them got up and stood around while we sang. I went with Miss Spence as she went from cot to cot talking to the wounded soldiers and Reds personally. They seemed very eager for the gospel and some followed us from ward to ward to hear more. We praise the Lord for the opportunity given to visit the hospitals three afternoons a week.

The Bible Conference was on at Nanchang so there were many meetings to attend. On Sunday a number of Chinese followed the Lord in baptism. The evangelist must have seen pictures of baptisms in Africa where they wear helmets because he wore his felt hat while he baptized. We might have laughed had we not been forewarned. In the afternoon, two bus loads of us, including those who were baptized, went out to the Leper hospital for a service. We sat on the one side of the church and the lepers sat on the other. The faces of some of them were nearly eaten off by this dread disease. At the close of the meeting a number stood up to signify that they wanted to decide for Jesus. Coming back from the hospital, we passed hundreds and hundreds of fresh graves of government soldiers and Reds who have been killed in recent fighting.

Prior to moving on to Kweiki and to escape the hot summer months, Florence and the family travelled to Yükiang (Anjen).

> For the hot summer months, Mr. Lewis, our Superintendent, has decided that we go to Yükiang (Anjen) and then proceed to Kweiki, our permanent station, in the Fall. Both stations are on the Kwangsin River. On May 23rd we left Nanchang in a small Chinese launch. Our cabin was very small and contained a table, stool, and three narrow benches on which to sleep. The first night things were too "lively" to sleep, but the next night we outwitted the bugs by putting our bedding inside our mosquito nets, thus closing us all in, and burning the lantern all night. The scenery along the river was delightful—lovely large trees, green fields, and towering mountains. Miss Huntamer met us here at Anjen and took us up to the C.I.M. compound. The house here is very large and will be much cooler for the baby and ourselves during the heat. There is, however, very little furniture because the soldiers have been occupying the house and have destroyed and burned nearly all the furniture. We are reminded time and time again that fine furniture does not make a home; it is only the presence of Jesus in our midst.
>
> Please continue to pray for us as we stay here. During the day our time will be taken up with language study and in the evening we intend to visit the homes and hand out tracts.

A few weeks after arriving, however, there was severe flooding in the area which deposited two feet of water in the Mission Home and eight feet in the Chapel. The flood conditions necessitated a move for the young family to Kuling, Kiangsi, a mountainous resort.

VIII

Kuling

Lord, who shall abide in thy tabernacle? who shall dwell in thy holy hill? He that walketh uprightly, and worketh righteousness, and speaketh the truth in his heart. (Psalm 15:1–2)

To get to Kuling, the Paulsons had to travel back to Kiukiang and then to the foot of the 4,836 foot high Mount Lu. From there they had to proceed along a steep, narrow stone stairway circling the outside of the mountain in an ever ascending climb to Kuling. It was an exhausting, arduous, three hour journey, comprising a steep twelve mile long path of more than a thousand steps. Coolies[19] were hired to carry the luggage hung from one end of a pole and young Philip in a basket from the other end, and sedan chairs for Florence and Cliff.

The path up the mountain was called the "Thousand Steps," but the Chinese called it the "Strong or Brave Man Steps," as only the strongest men could handle the ascent to Kuling. Usually six coolies were assigned to a sedan chair, four to carry and two for relief.

In her autobiography, *My Several Worlds,* Pearl Buck describes the ascent up the mountain with her mother: "We seated ourselves in our chairs and four bearers carried each chair, suspended by ropes from poles across their shoulders, and thus they mounted the first flight of stone steps with light rhythmic stride. Up the mountain we climbed . . . . The road wound around the rocky folds of the cliffs and beneath us were gorges and rushing mountain rivers and falls. Higher and higher the road crawled, twisting so abruptly that sometimes our chairs swung clear over the precipices as the front bearers

---

[19] The Chinese word for Coolie means "bitter strength." On relatively flat terrain and carrying one or two passengers, a coolie can travel at the rate of six or seven miles an hour running with only a few breaks from sun-up to well past dusk.

went on beyond the rear ones, still behind the bend. One misstep and the chair would have been dashed a thousand feet into the rocks and swirling waters, but there was never a misstep. In all the years I never heard of an accident, even though the bearers went at an astonishing speed, every step in rhythmic movement. Somewhere near the top of the mountain we turned a certain corner and were met . . . by a strong cold current of mountain air. Until then the air had gradually cooled, but at this spot it changed suddenly and the bearers welcomed it with loud hallooing calls and a spurt of running, the chair swaying between them." (p. 131)

The Chinese considered Mount Lu to be a sacred mountain. Situated amongst a series of mountains, it was majestic and rugged, with its upper regions often shrouded in mist and fog. Nestled 3,500 feet up the mountain is Kuling. With its air cooled by forest breezes, it was an excellent place for Florence and the family to escape the stifling heat on the plains. The town was ideal. It had numerous facilities and most amenities. And the houses were beautiful, built with grey stone and covered with various coloured clay tile roofs, some painted green, others red or black. Close by were famous sites, and everywhere was breathtaking scenery and expansive views of the Yangtze River and the valleys below.

The Paulsons stayed in housing on the grounds of Chiang Kai-shek's summer palace,[20] with access to its spacious lawns and gardens. The days went quickly, with picnics and visits to the enchanting waterfalls and ancient Chinese temples.

After a wonderful summer in Kuling, Florence wrote to her sister.

Kuling, Kiangsi
September 1, 1935

Dear Frances,

Received your letter also the papers, for which we thank you very much. How do you like the new government? I see by the China Daily that Aberhart was elected provincial premier. He hasn't got such a hard job as the Generalissamo of China. General Chiang Kai-shek and Madame Chiang came to their home here on Kuling but could only stay a day or two then they had to fly back

---

[20] Chiang Kai-shek's summer palace or villa was his official summer residence. It spanned an area of 1,200 square yards and was frequently used as a military training and marshalling area for the Nationalist army.

to Szechuan. The Reds seem to be worse in the North at present. Kansu is partially evacuated and also southern Shensi.

We have had a delightful summer here. I have pretty well finished studying the gospel of John in Chinese despite all the picnics and interruptions. We each got a month's ticket to the swimming pool so we have enjoyed a daily bath. We also had the pleasure of hearing the world famous Cossacks give their musical programme. We have visited most places of interest such as Nan K'an Pass,[21] Dragon Pool,[22] Three Trees,[23] Emerald Pool, Sunset Ridge, Pine Walk, etc., but best of all we have enjoyed the spiritual blessings. We have had the most interesting study in the Book of Hebrews by one of the Foreign Spiritual leaders of China, Mr. Graham by name. We also had a week's meetings on the Victorious Life, which were all spiritual treats. There were various Chinese Conferences with such outstanding men as Wang Ming Tao, Mr. and Mrs. Chao but from which we do not get full benefit because of our limited language.

September is here. Philip has grown a good deal this summer. This morning during prayers he was trying to pull up my skirt and Cliff's trouser legs to tickle our knees with a feather. He sings out loud whenever singing is going on. He took a notion to kiss everyone in the hall one day, even to the Chinese tailor. He loves to shake hands with everyone. Bogers have a tiny baby so he asks to see the shao baby. "Shao" means young in Chinese. He is quite a favorite around here with all his uncles and aunts.

We expect to go down Tuesday as to-morrow we will be busy packing all day. A person always collects a few extra things which one finds it hard to find room for. The Kiangsi Conference is from the 4th—12th of September so we will be staying in Nanchang for it. They say it is very hot on the plain so we will likely find it quite different to the coolness here.

There were 7 of us from Prairie Bible Institute here at Kuling one day. We had a picnic together. It is nice to meet those again with whom we went to Bible School. Four of them were up here for two weeks or more. We took some snaps of the group. We go on one picnic every week unless rain prevents us and sometimes more often. The scenery is very beautiful. From the heights

---

[21] Nan K'an Pass is a mountain pass between the rugged peaks of Lion's Leap and the softer slopes of the Hanyang Mountains. The pass allows an extensive view of Poyang Lake and the old city of Nanchang.

[22] Dragon Pool and Emerald Pool were beautiful mountain pools fed by several waterfalls where the young family picnicked and swam.

[23] Three Trees is the site of two gigantic cedars and one ginkgo tree planted by monks during the Ming Dynasty (1368–1644).

we can see the Yangtze River, Poyang Lake,[24] rice fields, cities of Kui Kiang and Singtze.

Cliff and Ed Cary are going on an errand to American Schools this afternoon so I think Philip and I will go along for the walk. There is a large shopping district here, 3 or 4 churches, a Chinese and 2 Foreign Schools, 2 or 3 hospitals, 2 swimming pools, 4 or more tennis courts.

Cliff is having a rest and Philip is rolling his socks down or taking them off and on. He loves to try and dress himself. He can put his trousers, shoes and socks on. He usually wants to put his waists and sweaters on by his feet also. I must close for now. I trust this finds you all well. May God richly bless you all.

With love from us all,
Florence, Cliff and Philip

---

[24] Poyang Lake is the largest freshwater lake in China. It contains numerous islands edged by white sands, and pagodas and temples situated on some of the islands.

IX

Kweiki

Gracious Spirit, dwell with me! I myself would gracious be;
And with words that help and heal would thy life in mine reveal;
And with actions bold and meek would for Christ my Saviour speak.[25]

In the fall of 1935, the family travelled from Kuling to Nanchang to attend a Christian conference. From there they travelled eighty miles to their first posting at Kweiki in Kiangsi Province. Kweiki is situated in a very mountainous and sparsely populated region of China.

In January of 1936, Florence wrote to her sister.

Kweiki, Kiangsi
Jan 13, 1936

Dear Frances,

Received your welcome letter. Cliff is away at a meeting of the Church Leaders to-night, to decide on special services for the Chinese New Year Season and Philip is in bed, so I have it nice and quiet. It is raining outdoors so it makes home more cheerful. Cliff is back already. The Chinese eat two meals one at 10 a.m. then another at 4 p.m., so they come to meetings about 6 p.m. so they are over early. They have their Chinese tea and sweets before the meeting begins, so they don't take long over having a social time.

We are still receiving Christmas cards from various friends.

Philip reminds me of Alex[26] when he used to say he had a headache, if he didn't want to eat a certain food. Philip says he has 3 stomachs. He calls the front of his neck one stomach, the back of his neck his small stomach, and his stomach his big stomach. He loves to say his prayers at night now. He says grace at the table but is not so keen on saying it every day. We don't make him

---

[25] Hymn: "Gracious Spirit, Dwell With Me," by Thomas Lynch.
[26] Alex is Florence's nephew, Frances' son.

say it unless he wants to. The Chinese coolies carry loads on a pole across their shoulder like they do at home, only here they have a song they sing as they jog along. Philip marches around the table with his elephant tied on a stick and he sings hi-ho-hi-ho. The women have a special song they sing their babies to sleep with also.

We had a very nice Christmas. We spent the day with the ladies, then they came to us for New Years. There are no turkeys here so we had roast chicken for Christmas dinner. We had a lovely dinner but we did not have real plum pudding, Christmas cake, nuts, apples, dates, figs, etc. We can't get any of those things unless we send to Shanghai for them. We get all kinds of jap oranges, persimmons, honeyed dates, but that is all the fruit we can get just now.

I took my first meeting here Sunday. I have to speak at the Children's Sunday afternoon service every 5th Sunday. There were about 35 children and 7 adults out. There would have been more if it hadn't been raining hard at that time. Cliff has his turn in teaching the Young Men's Bible class. We are very busy studying these days. The Chinese are all busy getting ready for their New Year which is a week from this Friday. There are quite a few visitors these days as the country Christians and non-Christians are all in town doing their shopping and settling accounts.[27] Most of the Christians call here when in town.

It has rained for nearly 2½ months now, so we don't get out very much these days. Our days are so full that we don't have time to notice the weather very much but we do like to take a walk each day it is fit to go out. Cliff may be away again in March with Mr. Glazier, who will be holding special meetings at Yuchan and Shangjao. He is busy at his books now. He is studying Matthew and I am studying Old Testament History. This part of China is quite peaceful at present. The communists are most troublesome in Hunan and Sezchuan.

You ought to see Philip with his chopsticks. He wants to use them everyday. He gets plenty to eat with them and it isn't that he has seen anyone use them very often. Rice and mien are two favorite foods of his. Well I can't think of much news.

May God bless and keep you all,
Your loving sister, Florence

Florence at this time was pregnant with her second child. Early in the spring, she travelled to Shanghai to have the baby. On May 31, 1936, Louise Elaine was born. Later, the family travelled once again to Kuling for the summer months.

---

[27] In China, all debts are to be settled before New Year's.

X

Hokow

And the things that thou has heard of me . . . the same commit thou to faithful men, who shall be able to teach others also. (2 Timothy 2:2)

After another wonderful summer at Kuling, the family proceeded to a new mission station at Hokow, in Kiangsi Province, where Cliff was to be in charge. It was the fall of 1936.

The mission's policy was to put an experienced missionary in charge of a station or central place, with one or two other supporting missionaries. At Hokow, Florence was the supporting missionary, but in evangelical work she was on equal footing with Clifford. From the central station, missionary service would be extended to the surrounding countryside and villages or outstations. Placement at a station was called a "posting." Invariably, all postings were inland and tended to be quite isolated from other foreigners. Missionaries were expected to stay a few years at one station—long enough to preach the gospel and help the Chinese Christians set up their own church and gospel outreach.

Cliff wrote a mission report detailing their arrival in Hokow and the commencement of their Christian work.

> "OH LOOK! Some new foreigners have come!"
>
> As we unloaded our household things from a long, brown river boat in the drizzling rain, the people sat just inside their doorways discussing the fact that some new foreigners had come to town, and commenting upon each article of furniture, or each box that was carried through the water from the boat to the long sloping sandy bank. They were especially interested in a little three-wheeled cart with a horse's head of bright red which we had brought with us from Kweiki for the children.

"They must have children," they would remark, as they poked their heads out of the doorways of their low, stuffy buildings. "Look at that small wheelbarrow."

Hokow, a busy little market city on the south bank of the lazy Kwangsin River, has a population of about thirty thousand. It is a center for the making of boats and rope. From our compound we look across a long stretch of open country to the foothills and high mountain ranges of Fukien Province. On the north lie the irregular, humpy, red rock hills. The city affords every opportunity for Gospel work, and the people are friendly and receptive.

Although we have been here but a month (October 1936), we have had tokens of God's gracious working. The Lord has sent a godly young man, Ho Hsing-tao, to help in the work. Mr. Ho has been on the teaching staff of the Bible Institute at Nanchang for five years. No man's preaching is a more faithful exposition of the Word of God, and his Gospel messages are both stirring and powerful. The church attendance has climbed to nearly one hundred, and a good number of these have recently become interested in the Gospel. We have visited the homes of all the old Christians on the street, in an effort to get many of them back into fellowship with God and His Son, Jesus Christ.

A young Christian, Mr. Teh, told us we could use his shop front twice a week for open-air meetings at night, but the street is narrow and the large crowds cause congestion, so we have to invite the listeners into the chapel and finish the message there. Mr. Teh has brought a fine young man, formerly an ardent idolater, to the Lord, and he is busy inviting other friends out to worship on Sunday morning.

God has sent to us three fine young ladies who make up a preaching band, and they work in the city and surrounding districts. Miss Wu of Kuling, their leader, is only a young Christian, but she is a faithful, untiring worker. Over thirty women from the street have been reached already, and these have indicated their desire to turn from idols to serve the true and living God. They have been attending regularly the services on Sunday and the women's meeting on Thursday. Mrs. Paulson has been doing a great deal of city and village work with the preaching band.

Mr. Ho and I visited Hu Fang, one of our outstations[28] twenty miles to the south. We went to the homes during the day and held evangelistic

---

[28] Travel to the outstations often involved dreary treks on foot or by bicycle over rough terrain.

meetings in the Gospel Hall at night. During our stay at Hu Fang, we came in contact with the very interesting Miao tribespeople, who make paper from bamboo at their villages back in the mountains and bring it down to the plain to sell. We were told that these thousands of villages have never been reached with the Gospel message, and God has put it upon our hearts to go up into the mountains later this fall, in an effort to reach them.

A preaching band of three young men have come to us from the Bible Institute at Nanchang, and they are working in our districts in the south country.

Yesterday about fifty soldiers came into our compound to look around, see the little foreign children, and get a drink at our well. Mr. Ho invited them into the chapel and preached to them for twenty minutes. They listened well, and all accepted gospels and tracts after the meeting.

With such promises of harvest, let us look to God for a great reaping. To Him be all the glory!

Providing further details of their missionary activities, Florence wrote a mission circular to mission supporters in Canada:

China Inland Mission
Hokow, Kiangsi

Dear Friends at Home:

> "Let us hold fast the profession of our faith without wavering (for He is faithful that promised) and let us consider one another to provoke unto love and good works". —Hebrews 10:23, 24.

In my last circular, I told you about our new home at Hokow, so now I shall tell you a little of what we have been doing.

We had the women's preaching band with us until sometime in January, when they went home for the Chinese New Year. There were three women in the band, Miss Wu of Kuling, a fine earnest young lady, being the leader. We had hoped to have Miss Wu remain on until the Bible School in Nanchang opened for the Spring term, but she was called back to Kuling unexpectedly because of sickness in her home. I might mention that Miss Wu is the young lady who last summer heard a stirring message at Kuling by Wang Ming Tao (said to be the most eloquent of all Chinese preachers and playfully called the "Machine Gun" by his Chinese associates in Christian work on account of the explosive and torrential nature of his messages) on Christian Walk and immediately went home, sold all her "finery", got right with God and fully followed the Lord.

Last Fall, we had Mr. William Taylor for our Fall Conference when over sixty leaders and outstanding Christians from our country districts met together for prayer and study of the Word of God, Mr. Taylor spoke for five days on the prayer life of our Lord, and his messages were the means of much quickening in the lives of the Christians. Nineteen were baptized and received into Church fellowship on the Saturday.

Since our preaching band has left, Mrs. Ho, the evangelist's wife, and I have been carrying on the regular Thursday afternoon women's meeting. We now have a third church member who is willing to take a turn at leading a meeting.

In February, we had a short term Bible School here. Mr. Lewis, our superintendent gave the opening messages. Although the attendance was not large (an average of from ten to twenty at each class), those who took the time off from their work on their farms, etc., to study the Word of God were greatly blessed. Old Farmer Su, a short wrinkled old man slightly stooped who is full of the glory of the Lord, and his son stayed until the very last. He sat on the front seat at every meeting drinking in the Word and feasting his soul upon the good things of God. He had a rather unpleasant experience with the bandits in his home last Fall, but it has greatly strengthened him in the Lord. Mr. Ho, our fine young Bible teacher and pastor, gave messages on Daniel, James and Exodus. Mr. Paulson took a series of studies in the book of Genesis. Since these meetings, two young men have desired to go out preaching with Mr. Ho and Mr. Paulson. Both supply their own food and expense money.

From a study of the Word we believe this is God's method, a self-supporting ministry upon whom He lays the burden of the dark, needy peoples of our surrounding districts. Let each of us as workers be much in prayer that we do not keep the Chinese leaders and Christians from entering into all that God has for them and deprive them of the privilege of working and giving by our tendency to continually "spoon feed". Mr. Paulson tells the following story regarding the native worker being the hope of a mission field. "An oriental gentleman, after listening to an address from a native pastor, made this remark: 'Once a forest was told that a load of axe-heads had come to cut it down. It does not matter in the least, said the forest, for they will never succeed. When, however, it heard that some of its own branches had become handles to the axe-heads it said, Now we have no longer any chance'. So, said the man, as long as we had only foreigners to deal with we were safe; but now that everywhere our own countrymen are enlisted on their side, certainly our faiths are doomed". I am sure it is true that the Gospel never sounds so sweet to the people from any other lips as from that of their own people. One of the young men mentioned above went home after two weeks, but the other young man has since been on trips to four outstations and is now waiting until a tent comes for them to use in meetings at a place called Shih-Ch'i.

We now have a primary school on the compound with twenty three little scholars. Miss Liu, formerly a member of our preachband, is the teacher and the children receive daily Bible instruction. The attendance at Sunday School has greatly increased since school was opened. We made small cards for each pupil. If they come on time, listen quietly, repeat their verse and bring another child to Sunday school we give them a gold star. If they lack one of these requirements, we give them a red star, if they lack two, an orange star and so on. For a certain number of marks we give a prize.

On Sunday morning, I have a young women's class and Mr. Paulson takes the students and young men. All who come to my class can read so it helps me a good deal as I am by no means fluent in the language yet. Some in the class are young married women; the Chinese girls marry very young.

There is much cause for praise for the fact that God is opening up work among the tribes in the mountains south of here. From our south verandah we see a long range of high, purple mountains which run down into the province of Fukien. Among these mountains there are many tribes people who make their living by making a coarse yellow paper (made up into square sheets and packed in large bundles bound tightly with thin, bamboo strips) from the bamboo trees that grow on the mountain sides and deep ravines. As far as we can find out, these people have never been reached with the Gospel message. At a place called Cheng-Fang, an earnest Christian man and his family have long desired to get a work started making the necessary preparations about a small hall on the main street of the town. Crude, wooden benches are being made by a carpenter and the hall will be ready in a few weeks. Cheng-Fang lies at the foot of a large, towering mountain. The day Mr. Paulson and Mr. Ho were there the mountain was capped with a beautiful fresh fall of snow. The feathery, yellowish green bamboo trees stretching up the mountain side in a delightful patchwork effect; the silvery, sparkling streams falling down the rocky sides; the wide, lazy river flowing out into the surrounding plain and many rice fields, truly made a remarkable picture as they approached the little town on foot. The narrow, cobbled street was filled with people buying and selling in the prosperous-looking shops. Many of these were tribes people with their bundles of paper. A number had their heads bound with a flowery blue-and-white cloth and they were wearing leather Chinese top shoes. The tribes women do not bind their feet and spend their time working out in the open with the men, or carrying the bundles of paper, etc. to market. We passed a number of women on the road.

The Chinese do not celebrate birthdays every year as we do, but celebrate when the child is one month old, one year, ten years, twenty, thirty, etc. Last Thursday, I was invited to a feast in honor of a baby boy who was one month old. Two tables of guests were invited, one of women and one of men. We had the usual delicacies of pork, eels, mien, etc.

A letter has come from a friend asking some questions about China. Others may be asking the same questions so I will answer them here.

The evangelist who was halting between taking a salaried position or continuing in the Lord's work has decided to stay on and trust the Lord. We heard him testify last week how God had blessed him both spiritually and financially because of his step.

China is fast becoming modernized. Places like Shanghai, Hankow, Nanchang and other large centres have new sections which are much like cities at home and the old sections which are truly oriental. Inland here in Hokow there is an electric light plant and buses (oil burning), but otherwise things have not changed much. The city is very idolatrous. The women do their washing in the river or ponds, the houses are mud walls, dirt floors and tile roofed. The average person's food consists of rice and green vegetables three times a day.

Many have asked what we ourselves eat when at home. For breakfast we usually have millet or rice gruel and an egg; dinner—fish, pork or eggs with such vegetables as sweet potatoes, greens, Chinese cabbage, turnips, beans, and a pudding, with carrot or mock pumpkin pie on Sunday for a treat (made from melon); for supper, we usually have eggs, toast, dried fruit and tea. We get oranges and a sort of grapefruit, peaches, plums, Chinese pears (very hard) and persimmons in their seasons. Peanuts are very plentiful and can be obtained almost any time. Tea is also grown near here. Philip and I wear Chinese clothes but Mr. Paulson and Louise wear the foreign. Foreign goods can be bought in large centres. Leather shoes are made on the street here, but the Chinese for the most part wear homemade, cloth shoes.

Florence: A Missionary in China

There is another religious order here with a large school. They give away medicines, etc. and thus get a good number of adherents who come for what they can get. It is certain that they have no Gospel to preach and thus their work is built up because of institutional, educational efforts. It would be quite easy to get people to come to church for loaves and fishes; we want those believers who follow Christ because they realize their NEED OF HIM.

Since beginning this letter, we received the good news that God was sending us a new worker in a few weeks, a Miss Virginia Casper of Milwaukee, Wisconsin, U.S.A. You do not realize what a joy her fellowship is going to mean in our home; may the Lord bring her to this field of labor in the fullness OF THE blessings of the Gospel.

Please remember the following requests in prayer:

1. We need a good Bible woman.[29]
2. That the TRIBES south of here may be reached with the Gospel.
3. Continued help with the language.
4. That God will mightily work in our young people.
5. Miss Casper's coming to this centre.
6. The twenty three little school children on the compound.
7. Our own little ones, Philip and Louise.
8. That God will lead Mr. Paulson about future short term Bible Schools.
9. For those contemplating following the Lord in baptism soon.
10. For the whole Church of China.

Thanking you all for your many letters which are such an encouragement and help to us as we labor here in the vineyard, we remain

Yours for needy China,
Mr. and Mrs. C. T. Paulson.
F.P.

---

[29] Chinese Bible women acted as assistants to female missionaries and were the social intermediaries between the missionary and the Chinese women in rural areas.

XI

Letters from Hokow

The days they spent in Hokow were full. Florence and Clifford were busy with their Sunday school and church meetings, visits to homes and neighbouring villages, and distribution of tracts. Despite her hectic schedule, Florence still had the pleasure of a few social outings, which she detailed in a letter to her sister.

> An old woman gave a party for her 70th birthday to-day so Misses Cruickshank, Robertson[30] and myself were invited. This morning at 9 a.m. we had tea and mien. This afternoon we go for a meal. For tea we had peanuts, sunflower seeds, candy and sugar made in the form of an old man. We ate his head and left the rest. The mien was very good. Miss Robertson had never eaten it before so she wasn't so fond of it. Only women were invited so Cliff didn't go. I can see the cook preparing a chicken for to-morrow. We have been eating with the ladies for a few days. We will certainly miss them when they go. It is nice to have someone so handy. The other day Philip pulled the Chinese sideboard over on top of himself. He broke one vase but fortunately it didn't touch him. The corner of the sideboard caught him above the eye and cut it but it didn't amount to much more than a bad scare. The weather has cooled off some so it is quite comfortable now. The Bible woman is away in the country this weekend.
>
> Grannies[31] death was certainly a shock to us. I meant to write but since I didn't get to it I remembered you all in prayer that God would comfort your hearts knowing she is now where no pain or sorrow can

---

[30] Missionaries visiting from another station.
[31] Frances' mother-in-law.

harm her. The death of a saint is precious in God's eyes, just another gone home to be forever with our Lord.

In January, Cliff went to Shangjao to pick up Lilla Cully, a new worker to replace Miss Casper.

> Cliff left this morning to meet Miss Lilla Cully. Mr. Lewis changed workers sending Miss Casper to Tuchang and Miss Cully here. Miss Cully is engaged to Mr. Brown who was here last fall for a week. The train comes in to Shangjao at midnight so he will be staying there overnight then coming back by bus to-morrow afternoon. I have had a good many interruptions this afternoon so that I haven't got much studying done. Yesterday we did a lot of moving things around preparing for Miss Cully to come. A Mr. McRoberts wants to come here for two months. If Mr. Lewis gives him permission we will let him come. He has been living on Chinese food for 7 mos. so needs a change. He is going to Kuling in July. Philip wants Cliff to bring him some blocks back from Shangjao.

Further updates on the family were provided to her sister, Frances, and her mother.

Hokow, Kiangsi
January 23, 1937

Dear Frances,

We have just come in from the evening service and as it is early I will write a few lines before retiring. The church is just in front of the house so we have no distance to go. We started or rather re-organized the Sunday school this A.M. We only had 14 out but that is a fair beginning. It rained most all week but the sun shone to-day. We had a Chinese lady from one of the out stations in to-day. She speaks very good English. She lost everything but her clothes when Hangchow was taken. She had two boxes of valuables when she left but they were put on the wrong boat so she lost them too. Her husband died last year. She has one daughter four or five years old. Next Sunday is the Chinese New Year. We have to serve tea to all the guests. We haven't prepared but we will have to this week. We serve melon seeds, peanuts, sugar candy and Chinese sweets. The damp atmosphere makes all the sweets melt so everything has to be kept in kangs of lime to keep them dry and crisp.

Florence: A Missionary in China

The children are in bed. Elaine has a sore eye to-day. It is very easy to get sore eyes in this country. She and Philip play well together. She loves to go out for a walk. The fire is roaring so it is quite cozy in here. We haven't had any snow yet this winter. The situation seems fairly peaceful here just now. Each ten homes has to provide one soldier and give $20.00 a month for his keep. Students are going all over to get the people to arise and use every means to save the country. We were having "mien" in a shop Friday when a couple came in. They spoke to us in English. They had been walking for 2 mos. and lecturing.

I feel sleepy after coming in from the cold. I wrote my 3rd exam and Lilla her second. We visited five homes last week. We are not getting mail very fast these days. We haven't had a newspaper for 2 days. Lilla's mother sent Elaine a little book of Bible stories. Anything in envelopes comes through and some newspapers but only very small parcels have been received. I sent a circular letter to Hankow to be printed so you will receive one eventually.

Cliff is here at the table reading a commentary on Corinthians. Lilla is in her room writing letters. She has a small heater in her bedroom so she writes in there. Her future husband may come over for the Chinese New Year. He couldn't leave the station to come over for Christmas. They are getting married early in June. The other missionary who was first appointed here is also getting married in June. June is a popular month for C.I.M. weddings. They can go away for the summer then. This time or a bit later last year our Supt. was with us but he won't be with us this year. He has been sent to Hankow for a time. I haven't received only a couple Christmas letters as yet but I hope there are more coming. We may get them next Christmas.

It is cold and rainy to-day. I want to write two more letters for the post to-day so I must close now. Trust you are all well. Philip is building a house out of boxes. Elaine has a craze for writing. She decorates the walls at times.

May God bless you all this New Year. We ordered calendars for our friends and relatives but they never came.

Your loving sister, Florence
Cliff and the kiddies send love.

M. J. Paulson

Hokow, Kiangsi
January 27, 1937

Dear Frances,

Thanks for your welcome letter and the little cloth book for Philip. Louise likes to look at it too. Philip had two white rabbits given to him. He squeezed one to death and I hurt the other by opening the door on it so that both are now dead, but since Philip has the picture of the rabbits in his book he says he still has some bunnies.

I led the women's meeting this afternoon. I spoke on Noah's Ark, Gen. 6 & 7. Two men and 8 women were present. It is unusual for men to come but when they come we can't turn them away. Philip is here playing at eating supper. Louise is in her basket. I am still nursing her. She has just had her supper. The Chinese are all getting ready for New Years. We had a present of eggs and rice cakes given to us this week. It is warm out to-day. We went for a walk down by the river. Philip gives away tracts to almost all whom we meet. To a few he says "they are not green so he won't give them one". I don't know what he means by green. One time he said "that man has black shoes so I will give him one". Cliff is busy reading the newspaper. We are still reading Chinese with a teacher, at least Cliff is, my teacher had to go home last week so I have had a weeks holiday from reading with the teacher but have been doing some studying. I am on Genesis just now. It is easy to study in Chinese. I was studying Romans but found it hard. We took some snaps of the kiddies to-day. Louise will be 8 mos. old on Sunday.

I haven't received mother's Christmas parcel yet. I wrote to Gladys[32] last week. Cliff does all the business correspondence and leaves me the personal letters so I have quite a few letters to write. His mother has been sick with gall stones. The doctor gave her lemon juice to dissolve the gall stones so she didn't have to have an operation. Cliff was out to a Chinese meal yesterday but they didn't ask me. He has been out to seven Chinese meals since we came to Hokow and I have been to four. I was bridesmaid at a Chinese wedding. I had to help dress the bride. Miss Wu was also a bridesmaid. The bride wore blue silk trousers, red[33] silk blouse, over which she wore a rented red embroidered shirt and coat, the worse for wear. On her head she wore the heavily beaded head piece. After the service she left in a chair carried by four men, with her

---

[32] Florence's second-oldest sister.
[33] Red is the standard wedding colour for brides in China.

face veiled, to go to her husband's home, where the real marriage ceremony would take place.

There isn't much news. There is the weekly services, visitors and the daily household affairs apart from them we usually take a short walk each day and read a little in the evenings. The kiddies go to bed at seven so we have a nice evening. Louise just got two teeth this week. She is a much better baby than Philip and he wasn't too bad. The Chinese are very fond of Philip. They prefer boys to girls. Many a girl baby is slain in the country districts. Philip can speak a good deal of Chinese now. There is a little Chinese children's hymn which says "To Respect your parents is very important". Philip sings it so that it means to respect your parents is not important. Philip has two little goldfish but since he can't handle them he doesn't pay much attention to them. He takes Louise's rubber doll to bed with him every night. I will have to get him a teddy bear sometime. The cheapest is $5.00 in Shanghai so I don't think we will buy one there.

I must close and put the kiddies to bed now.

Love to all from us all.
Your loving sister, Florence

Hokow, Kiangsi
April 27, 1937

Dearest Mother:

Louise can sit up from a lying down position now without any help. She does a lot of jabbering but only says da-da. We can buy fresh peas on the street now so we are enjoying green peas. The carrot season is over. We had it cold and wet for a few days. It will soon be Cliff's birthday then Louise's then mine. It is my turn to take the women's meeting this week but I am going to ask Mrs. Ho to take it if she will as I will have no time to prepare. I have three letters I want to get off so I will soon close. I planted some tomatoes in a box. They are growing but my lettuce hasn't come up at all. We have some beautiful large pink roses in the garden. They are very fragrant. I will put some in Miss Cully's room to-morrow. I am enclosing $1.00 bill. It will buy you something for Spring.

May God bless you,
Your loving daughter,
Florence

XII

War with Japan

For the Chinese people under Japanese rule, life meant death and dying meant torture.

In the 1930s, Japan's expansionist goals threatened China. Already in control of Manchuria, Japan moved into Mongolia and North China. No war had even been declared. In July of 1937, near Peking, the Nationalist government finally fought back. Despite their efforts, by August 1937 Peking and its seaport neighbour Tientsin had fallen. Japan then commenced an attack on Shanghai, establishing a naval blockade along the Chinese coast from Tientsin to Hong Kong, paralyzing China's foreign trade. By taking the coastal seaport cities, Japan hoped to subdue China by strangulation.

By November 1937, Shanghai had fallen. In December, the Japanese marched into Nanking,[34] the capital of the Nationalist government. In retreat, Chiang Kai-shek moved his government 340 miles inland along the Yangtze to Hankow. Then, when Hankow was taken in 1938, he moved his government a further 560 miles to Chungking in Szechuan Province.

---

[34] The atrocities committed by the Japanese army on the Chinese people in Nanking are referred to as "The rape of Nanking." Soldiers, who surrendered in the city, were executed in mass simply because they were too many to guard and feed. Often they were mutilated before death or killed in the most horrific manner—doused with gasoline and set on fire; buried alive or up to their chests and then trampled by horses, run over by tanks, or attacked by German Shepherd dogs. These atrocities were all in contravention of the 1929 Geneva Convention, Treatment of Prisoners of War. The civilian population fared no better. Chinese men were sodomized and used for bayonet practice. Women and female children were gang raped, while the more unfortunate ones were required to serve as prostitutes, one for every fifteen to twenty men, until they were too diseased to continue using and were killed or died from their experience. Then there were the Japanese soldiers who held contests as to who could behead the most people in a certain period of time, with claims of over a hundred apiece. The cruelty and savagery were unimaginable, including the slitting of children's vaginas so sexual relations could be more easily achieved. This killing spree continued for more than six weeks, with the death toll numbering an estimated 300,000 Chinese citizens, far more than the 200,000 killed by the atomic bombs dropped on Hiroshima and Nagasaki in 1945.

Inland, the Japanese advanced according to a predictable pattern along railway corridors, moving along the line from Peking into North Honan and from Tientsin into Soochow. Once Shanghai was taken, they advanced up the Yangtze along the east-west railway line.

Prior to moving into an area, the Japanese would engage in blitzkrieg bombing numerous times a day. This strategy provided the Japanese with a tactical advantage, terrifying the civilian population so that there was limited resistance when ground troops arrived.[35]

The Chinese people fled before the invasion. It's estimated the refugees numbered between 25 and 40 million. Margaret Crossett, a CIM missionary stationed in Anhwei, described the exodus:

> Day after day the refugees came, some with limbs missing where they had been struck by fragments of bombs; some the sole survivors of large families. . . . Men, women, and children tramped with bundles of bedding and clothing on their backs, or loads of things in baskets hung from poles across their shoulders. . . . By evening the city was as the city of the dead. . . . Carpenters could not make coffins fast enough to bury the dead, and many bodies were thrown outside the city for the pigs, dogs, and vultures to dispose of. (Austen, p. 250)

Providentially, Florence and her young family were a considerable distance southwest of the fighting. However, with Shanghai taken by the Japanese and the conflict in that area, supplies normally obtained from Shanghai could no longer be procured. In a mission circular, Florence documented a few of the minor hardships imposed by the war.

CHINA INLAND MISSION
Hokow, Kiangsi

January 21, 1938

Dear Friends:

No doubt many of you at home will be wondering just how much the present troubles in China are affecting us. Apart from a few inconveniences we cannot

---

[35] The Japanese also trafficked in opium, promoting its sale and consumption amongst the Chinese to help finance the Japanese army and weaken the Chinese people's will to resist. They also introduced germ warfare—cholera, typhus, anthrax, bubonic plague—in an attempt to create epidemics amongst the population.

say they have affected us to any great extent, but if the war zone extends to here just what will happen is difficult to foretell. In the first place, the unsettled conditions and disruption of communications made it impossible for us to leave the hill resort (Kuling, Kiangsi) in August as we had planned, but we finally arrived back home on September 11th. Since that time the bus and railway service has been greatly hindered by existing hostilities; it is almost impossible for us to get foodstuffs and supplies from Shanghai. We depend on Shanghai for such things as salt, baking powder, spices, hymnbooks, clothing, lamp glasses, etc. Being cut off from Shanghai makes us more resourceful in using local products and it is now necessary for us to refine the coarse, dirty salt bought locally, purify the sugar and find out various ways of using rice and vegetables. Flour, coal-oil, sugar and butter are very expensive, but rice and garden products are quite cheap.

So much for food problems. Just received a Christmas card yesterday so you can guess the rest, but please don't let that keep you from writing; we get the letters eventually and we need word from home more than ever in these times. If we don't take our required amount of exercise we make up for it now when we take a trip to the country; since there are no busses, walking is preferred to taking a native wheelbarrow[36] over the rough stones. Aeroplanes from the front lines fly over occasionally. The deep vibration of the engines foretells their deadly errand. One day a plane circled over our church building so low that the pastor was so frightened he forgot his sermon.

Last Tuesday on a trip to the country I was encouraged to see the number who asked for tracts. We used to give out tracts wholesale, but lately it has come to us that it is much wiser to carry tracts and just offer them to one or two persons—the others will ask for them. This day quite a number called after us for the tracts. On the boat as we crossed the river a woman asked many questions about the Gospel and as we were travelling the same direction Miss Liu, our teacher, took advantage of the opportunity to show her the way of Life. Since the outbreak of hostilities between China and Japan people seem ready and eager for something so now is our chance to give them the Truth. There has been an opportunity to give the gospel to the educated classes as never before; many of the universities and colleges are now closed and the students and teachers are at home. Please pray that the Word may fall upon prepared hearts.

---

36 A Chinese wheelbarrow consists of a platform atop one wheel, pushed with two handles. The Chinese believe that the louder the wheelbarrow squeaks the better, because then it will bring good luck. Travel by wheelbarrow was very uncomfortable due to road conditions, as the wheelbarrow would bump along slowly, jarring the passenger.

M. J. Paulson

At present we have about twenty refugees from Chekiang living on our compound. They belong to the wealthy, educated class; a few of them are teachers from the Presbyterian school at Chia Hsing, Chekiang. A few of them are earnest Christians. We trust the Lord has led them here for good. They have been travelling for more than three months fleeing from the approaching armies. They have children and servants with them; it reminds one of the moving of the children of Israel in O. T.[37] times. Jacob couldn't travel fast because the children were young.

This year about fifty had asked for baptism. A number of these were young men, however, and were afraid to venture out for fear of being taken to be soldiers. Thirty-three followed the Lord in baptism; this is an increase over last year. Mr. William Taylor was with us again last November for the Fall conference. The numbers were fewer than the year previous but there was a fine spirit in all the meetings. The Bible studies from Revelation and John, and the messages on "Church Deportment" and "What the Bible teaches about War" were most helpful. The church leaders and local Christians presented Mr. Taylor with a hand-painted box and a holder for Chinese sweetmeats. Mr. Taylor and Mr. Paulson went from here to Shangjao, 80 li[38] away for meetings. During the meetings here, one evening was given to a discussion of the ways and means of promoting family worship in the homes. There are a few in our district who are faithful to maintain daily family worship and we trust and pray that the number of such homes will increase.

For those who haven't heard from us since our Spring circular, I might mention Miss Liu's special meetings in June. She is one of the Bible teachers at the Nanchang Bible School. The meetings were well attended by the city people but the country folks were unable to come in because it was so near feast time. There was a flood at the time delaying her visit to the army camp. Mr. Ho and the others were able to give Gospel messages at the camp and distribute about 500 portions of the Word.

Because Miss Brown and Miss McFarlane of Shangjao were not permitted to go back to their station after the summer due to Miss McFarlane's health, their station was left without a missionary. The soldiers constantly threatened to occupy the premises so Mr. Paulson had to make a number of trips there to look after the work. It was after the middle of November before Miss Cully and I had our first trip to the country. The Saturday we left for Ien Shan was warm so we enjoyed the 30 li tramp through beautiful scenery with

---

[37] Old Testament.
[38] A li is 1/3 of a mile.

mountains, trees and rivers. We stopped to explore a cave and Miss Cully just escaped stepping on a poisonous snake. At Ien Shan, crowds flocked to see us and to watch us eat. Mr. Ch'en the Chinese evangelist took advantage of his many opportunities to give those who came a chance to hear the Gospel. Since it was the first time I had left Elaine,[39] I thought I had better not be away too long, so we returned by boat on the Monday.

Our next trip was longer both in distance and time. We took wheelbarrows[40] but walked a good part of the way. The day was very warm and although I started out wearing a wadding I soon shed it. At Hu Fang, our station, the pastor, his mother and one of the deacons met us on the edge of the city so we were given a warm welcome. We attended a wedding and a birthday feast, both occasions giving splendid opportunities for Mr. Ho to preach the Gospel. I heard the people on the street remark, "Is she a man or a woman". At a Chinese wedding, a feast is given at the bride's home the evening before the wedding day, then again the next day for breakfast and dinner. Both evening and the wedding afternoon services are held in the bride's home. After the second service the bride gets into a sedan chair sent by the bridegroom and proceeds to the bridegroom's home where the actual wedding ceremony takes place. The bride's parents do not witness the ceremony, only one of the family, usually a brother of the bride, goes with her. The guests at both homes for the most part are not the same; in this case there were 160 guests at both homes. After the ceremony we again partook of a feast, then returned to the city. In the morning just after daybreak, sedan chairs arrived from the bridegroom's home to take us back there. The guests usually remain over night but we preferred to go back to our little room above the School rather than sleep in the room with all the other guests. The cooks and helpers worked day and night to prepare food for all the guests. When we arrived at the bridegroom's home the next day, tea was served, then later the breakfast. After breakfast a Gospel service was held after which the bride's boxes were opened and her garments counted. It is the custom in China that the bride has to provide a certain number of garments, pieces of furniture, etc. when the engagement is arranged. After the boxes were put away 60 pairs of Chinese cloth shoes and stockings were put on the table by the bride to be distributed among the guests. I received a pair of blue brocaded ones but they are hardly long enough for my number 6's. After the noon meal we all dispersed.

---

[39] For some reason, Florence started calling Louise by her second name, Elaine.
[40] Travel in the rural areas typically consisted of wheelbarrows, bicycles, or walking. In the cities it was by sedan chair or rickshaw for the wealthy.

I haven't space to tell of our visit to two other villages, suffice it to say that we find after visiting the Christians they are always much more friendly and more regular in their attendance at Sunday services.

We don't know what this year has in store for us but we do know that He is on the Throne and that all things work together for good to them that love the Lord. You will glean from these pages items for prayer, but for convenience I will group them as follows:

Pray for—
1. The educated classes who are home.
2. The Sunday-school which we have just re-organized.
3. The Young People in public and high schools.
4. Guidance in times of danger.
5. That the war might be brought to a close.
6. Those in authority in the Government and the Mission.
7. Guidance as to the Spring work.
8. That a Bible woman might be raised up to
9. help in the work among women.
10. For the 33 baptized this year, that they might be strong in the Lord.

Yours sincerely,
FLORENCE PAULSON.

P.S. Philip's chief enjoyment now is playing coolie. He kisses Elaine "goodbye", packs everything imaginable into his little grip and basket, picks up his little carrying pole and away he goes. Elaine's choice words are "ago" for orange and "walk". When she first opens her eyes in the morning she says, "Mummy, ago walk".

XIII

Shanghai

Take my yoke upon you, and learn of me; for I am meek and lowly in heart: and ye shall find rest unto your souls. (Matthew 11:29)

In the fall of 1938, Florence and the children went to Shanghai because of guerrilla unrest around Hokow, while Cliff went to Nanchang to help with the work there. Typically, when there was turmoil in the countryside, the women and children were moved to the coast for safety.

Now that Shanghai had been completely secured by the Japanese army, travel there was possible. The Chinese Nationalists had been pushed into the south and west parts of the country, called Free China, while Japan held most of the major coastal cities and the lines of communication: the railways. Small bands of Chinese guerrillas operating in areas within Japanese-occupied territory would attempt to disrupt Japanese operations by attacking blockhouses or blowing up ammunition trains. The problem with this, however, was that reprisals by the Japanese army were always enacted against the civilian population.

As Japan was not yet at war with the Allies, Florence and the children could safely travel to Shanghai. Florence wrote her sister from the mission compound in Shanghai, where she was hospitalized for rheumatism in her legs.

1531 Sinza Road
Shanghai, Kiangsu
February 1, 1939

Dear Frances,

Received your welcome letter sometime ago also the books. I was waiting to receive the gift of money before writing. I received it this A.M. Thank you all ever so much for the gift and books.

The kiddies enjoyed the cut-out pictures. The books they take to bed with them most nights. Elaine especially wants me to tell her the story of each picture, over and over again. She nearly always wants Philip's books too. She is especially fond of pictures of ducks.

I am in the hospital for a few days with rheumatism. It sounds worse than it really is because at home we would have to be very sick before we went to hospital but here we have our C.I.M. hospital on the top floor so if we have a very bad cold we can go to hospital if we like. Mrs. Eaton, a C.I.M. nurse, whose husband died here in Oct. is looking after Philip & Elaine. They come and see me twice a day. It is all in the same building so I don't seem very far away from them. They are happy and haven't made any fuss. I hope to go downstairs to Maybeth Judd's wedding Friday. She is marrying Ken Gray of Calgary. I think I will let Philip & Elaine see the wedding as they love Auntie Maybeth, but they can't go to the reception. There are two cases of chicken pox among the children. We are not sure whether Elaine had them or not as her vaccination took very badly and just at that time she got what looked like blisters all over her, in her hair and even on the sole of her foot. I am trying to get my studying done so I can write my last exam this month. Cliff was here for Christmas & New Years. He went back on Jan 6th. Mr. & Mrs. Beard are at Hokow so he has someone to do the housekeeping. The children like it here, because they have little playmates. I had a lovely shell pink bed jacket given to me this morning, also a package of toffee. Yesterday, I had a bouquet of violets, and the day before a glass of orange juice, so you see everyone is very kind.

It has got very dark, it must be going to rain or snow. We have had a very warm winter so far. I have been moved into a room with another patient so we get talking and I don't get much accomplished. It seems needless to stay here. I sit up all day and can go to the bathroom but that is all the farther they will let me walk. The rheumatism was about 20 patches of inflammation on my legs. I thought it was boils. It got very painful to stand but wasn't bad when I walked. The inflammation is all gone now and only patches of bluish yellow remain, like bruises. I just had a bath and my afternoon cup of tea (milk & water) so now perhaps I can finish this letter. I will be glad when my exam is over so I can rest or work as I like. I want to get some of Philip's outfit ready for school. It sounds as if I am in a rush but when I go back Inland, I likely won't be back here for a long time so will have no chance to shop. I can get a camel's hair quilt made, pillow cases, sheets, dressing gown and those sort of things ready. It has been good for Philip to be here and mix with the other boys. The Chefoo children were here for nearly 2 months so he had many playmates. They all went back to school last Tuesday. It is quiet around here now. Elisabeth Hoyte is having a birthday party to-morrow so Philip & Elaine are looking forward to having ice cream. One of the women going back Inland didn't want to take very much with her so she gave Elaine a lovely rose coloured knitted dress which was too large for her little two year old as her child is very small for her age and Elaine is tall for her age. Elaine's hair is getting thick now. For a long time it was thin. It is still a little curly but not as much as before I cut it. There isn't much to write about. There is always someone coming & going but you wouldn't know any of them. Mr. Aldis the Home Director of England had a birthday yesterday so I came in for some birthday cake, yesterday & to-day. I have had a few visitors. The children will be up soon so that will be another hour of playing. So mother is back in Victoria. She would like Chinese winters, warm and rainy. I must close now. Thank you again for your kindness.

Your loving sister,
Florence

Florence stayed on at Shanghai for the delivery of her third child, Keith Beverly, born May 2, 1939.

Dear Frances,

Excuse stationary but all my paper is downstairs and I don't want to disturb Philip & Elaine. I suppose Mother has told about our big boy Keith Beverly. He is hollering his head off just now. He gained 7 oz. in 2 days so he can't be sustained. I have just had a typhoid inoculation so I hope it doesn't effect him. I don't care about being done but it is safest to be inoculated especially since I haven't been done for nearly five years. We had Philip & Elaine inoculated for diphtheria to-day. It is supposed to last a life time. There is little one can do for diphtheria if one got it Inland.

We are being sent to Kiangtu Kiangsu for 6 months. There is a lady doctor there belonging to the Baptist Mission. There are also Anglicans there besides seven of our missionaries. It is a large centre. We are to live in the Training Home so I expect it will be fairly cool being a large building with a through draft. There is a beautiful big garden for the children to play in and fruit trees. It is in the Japanese controlled area. The broach or rather clip is all the fashion in England now. You just clip it on the neck of any dress. I haven't had any more rheumatism. I am fine except a bit weak yet. The hospital is in the same building as the Mission Home but on the 5th floor. We pay the same board in both places so it costs no more to live in the hospital except for doctors and hospital supplies and medicines.

I have finished all my exams now. Cliff is to be studying while in Kiangtu. Cliff came here in April or the last of March to look after the children. He has still 2 more exams to do. I got 91% on my 4th which was 1% more than Cliff but he is better at the spoken than I am.

Cliff is at the Sat. prayer meeting. Yesterday was an all day of prayer commemorating the first party to land in China under C.I.M. I attended two meetings. There will be nine of us at Kiangtu so there will be enough to make a fair sized prayer meeting on Sat. which is our C.I.M. prayer meeting day throughout the Mission. In England they say there are two things punctual, the Big Ben and the C.I.M. prayer meeting. You will think this letter is from Aunt Pat for the kind of stationary[41] I am using but I just finished my paper I had here before writing to you. Some missionaries are going to Canada to-morrow so I will get them to take this. Cliff just came in. I must get this finished to-night as if the effects of the typhoid inoculation are very severe I may stay in bed to-morrow. It is handy to be in the hospital while having inoculations because one can have their meals sent to their room. Cliff is preaching at the Hut. to-morrow. He preached on the radio last Sunday. He has a few meetings a week either English or Chinese. I expect to go down Wed. to the Mission Home. I have had a good rest here. The first two weeks while I was in bed I read a good deal and just rested and enjoyed myself. I had fruit, candy, grape juice, flowers sent to me besides all kinds of things for baby. Baby received a silk pram cover & pillow, 2 pair woollen rompers, 1 pr of silk rompers, soap, shirt, jacket, stockings, shoes, 2 pr short socks. He has everything but a buggy, pillow, a mattress and a summer bonnet. I must close as my back aches and it is time for baby to eat.

Love from us all,
Florence, Cliff, Philip, Elaine & Beverly

---

[41] Florence's letter was written on the back of two postcards and brown wrapping paper all taped together.

XIV

Kiangtu

But whosoever drinketh of the water that I shall give him shall never thirst; but the water that I shall give him shall be in him a well of water springing up into everlasting life. (John 4:14)

In June of 1939, after Keith's birth and Florence's improvement in health, the family moved to Kiangtu or Yangchow, as it was formerly called, in Kiangsu Province. Located about 100 miles upriver from Shanghai, Yangchow was the CIM's language school for female missionaries. It was part of China, but occupied by the Japanese.

Florence wrote her sister a letter:

Kiangtu, Kiangsu
August 17, 1939

Dearest Frances, Alick & Family:

The war affects us as far as cost of living, danger of travelling and restrictions as to where we can go. We constantly hear firing in the country. I had a guest until supper time then we had supper after which I fixed up four vases of flowers two for the dining room and two for the sitting room. It began to rain so I had to come in. It is quite dark now. The evenings are getting in.

The rice crop is very poor here this year but good in Kiangsi. Philip and Elaine think Keith is just it. As soon as they are dressed they make a dive for the bed where Keith is and try to make him laugh. They both want to hold him. We have a folding buggy, a red one, for him. He spends most of his time on the verandah in it when he is not in bed. I don't allow the Chinese to carry him but they can wheel him around sometimes. We had our second cholera inoculation to-day so our arms are all a little sore. There is four cases of smallpox in the city so there is notices up for everyone to be vaccinated.

We had company so I didn't get this letter finished. It is now Monday. Mr. and Mrs. Springer & their 2 year old daughter, Mary Olive, came to Yangchow for the weekend staying with Mr. and Mrs. Glazier. Glazier's had a tea for them on Sat. afternoon at 4 p.m. We all went except Keith. They came over this morning to see this place before catching the 9 o'clock bus. To-day all the Chinese have to get their picture taken. It costs them 10 cents each. They certainly intend keeping close tab on everyone. It is all passes and searchings these days. We hope to have some snaps to send you next time. We took a film but haven't it developed yet. Baby is in bed. Elaine wants a knife. We just helped take some peaches off a tree. They are still green. We haven't had any peaches for a long time. We can only get apples and hard pears just now. We have pears nearly every day. We had a dessert made of milk and gelatine yesterday. Gelatine is nice on hot days. There is no ice here but things keep cool down the well. Keith is growing fast. I haven't weighed him for sometime though. I am making Elaine a navy spotted dress for cool days. Summer will soon be over. It has been a cool summer for China. The children have had very little prickly heat. We haven't slept on the verandah at all this summer.

Young men and missionaries on furlough are coming out this Fall but no young ladies. We don't know where they intend sending the men yet. We had company. Miss Sellon brought 4 sealed packages of good American coffee and a box of cookies so I provided the hot water, sugar and milk and we had a little tea party. Miss Lajus came over just in time for a cup. It tasted good. This morning seems to be a continual round of interruptions. I hear that postage is going up double, if so, I must get all my letters written. We had another guest. She has just gone now. Philip had me make him a belt. He loves to sew. He cuts out trousers and jackets and says he is making daddy a suit. He is very particular and loves to get cleaned up and is always wanting to change his suit. He has a white suit which he loves to wear. Elaine isn't at all particular. We call her sloppy Ann. We are late to-day. It is 12:15 and no dinner ready. We have breakfast at 7 a.m. so we are always ready for dinner. It is fortunate that we had morning coffee to-day. Elaine's canary sings now. She has the male bird and she named it Cherry. Philip has the female bird and he calls his Dickie. There are some stray cats around so Elaine catches them and brings them in the house. She loves cats but she is a bit rough with them. One cat is enough to keep. I must close now.

Ever your loving sister
Florence

Florence: A Missionary in China

Florence also wrote an open letter to Mission supporters in Canada:

Kiangtu, Kiangsu
August 22, 1939

Dear Friends:

These are very uncertain days as you all know and although missionaries have had many and varied experiences in China, we are living at a time when conditions are very different from those which have previously been experienced. As most of you know the children and I remained on in Shanghai last August. Mr. Paulson returning alone to Kiangsi. Mr. Paulson came back to Shanghai in March. After I left the C.I.M. hospital, where our second son, Keith Beverly, was born on May 2nd, we were asked to consider my remaining on in Shanghai while Mr. Paulson accompanied Mr. Birch to Anhwei. We did not feel it was the Lord's will for us so asked if we couldn't all go together to some place so here we are, living in the Women's Training Home at Kiangtu. Coming out married I went with the men to Hwaining so I never expected I would ever have the pleasure of a visit here.

Kiangtu or Yangchow, as it was formerly called, is a very old city. At one time it was a place of official residence, being one of the capitals of China. It was here that Marco Polo was received at Court. It is peopled mainly by wealthy people and is a very idolatrous city. As one walks down the streets he or she meets many counting their beads and occasionally one is seen on her knees praying. Next door to us is a Widows Home founded by wealthy Buddhists. In Yangchow it is a disgrace for a widow to re-marry. Kiangtu is on the grand canal. There is a lake and a few pretty spots, where one can go for a few hours pleasure, but I haven't been out to see them yet as it is too hot to take the children out during July and August. We arrived here June 15th.

We have had a comparatively cool summer, there being a breeze most days. This building was built under the supervision of Dr. Cox, who was born in India so it is well adopted for hot weather but cold in winter. We have a good-sized garden, and a lawn both at the back and front but it has been neglected for the past two years so is not as nice as it could be. We have an abundance of flowers though, supplying two other compounds besides what we use. There are eight of us C.I.M. missionaries in the city, Mr. and Mrs. Orr at South Gate. Mr. and Mrs. Glazier and Gracie at Central Hall, Misses Lajus and Sellon, who have charge of Skin-Market-Street Chapel and a Girls School. We have been sent here to study so have no definite church work, only to help where asked. Mr. Paulson has preached three Sundays, has a boys Sunday school class and helped in a twelve day Daily Vacation Bible School.

Three li from the city is a hill on which is a temple, where the famous Goddess of Mercy is. Every year, during July and August, pilgrims come from five provinces, to worship there. The various churches have gospel booths for giving forth the Word of Life. Mr. Paulson went for one day. Formerly pilgrims went in such great numbers that two nights the city gates were left open allowing the crowds to go day and night but this year there were very few visitors.

Some ask, "Is there any fruit from this widespread distribution of gospel literature?" Mr. Orr told me this story. A young man left the throng, on their way to the temple, and stepped inside the gospel booth. After partaking of the usual cup of tea he proceeded to examine the tracts on the table. He was given one, which he read then he asked for other kinds and was given one of each of the various leaflets. As he left, the missionary uttered a silent prayer that he might receive the Truth. The following year another crowd flocked to the temple for the yearly pilgrimage. This time an old woman stops at the gospel booth muttering. "This is the place", "Yes this is the place". She told this story. Last year my son came here and you gave him some pamphlets, which he took home and pasted up on the wall, reading them over and over again. One day, he cried, "I have it" "I have it". He tore down the idols telling me that they were false and that we must worship the one true God. He took sick and died but he died a happy death and he made me promise that when the time came for the yearly pilgrimage, that I would come here to you to learn more of the doctrine. You can be sure the missionary was glad to tell her the old, old, story "all have sinned" Rom. 3:23. "The wages of sin is death" Rom. 6:23. "He that believeth on the Son hath everlasting life and he that believeth not the Son shall not see life; but the wrath of God abideth on him" John 3:36.

Among the eighty odd children that attended the Daily Vacation Bible School, was a blind boy. The other boys teased him and tried to lead him the wrong way by taking his hand and saying, "this way," "this way," but he would answer "you are not my teacher for he is tall." One day a soft white hand was slipped into the blind boy's yellow-skinned one. The teacher whispered, "he will lead you upstairs to your class for he is my little boy." Day after day for the full twelve days the blind boy came and drank in the Word of God and learned to love and praise the Lord Jesus Christ. It was not easy for him to come because he had to feel his way, and his granny, (his own mother being dead) did not want the boy to leave the idols and worship the true God.

Florence: A Missionary in China

At last the day for the closing exercises came. The blind boy stood up and repeated the whole of the 23rd Psalm. Three weeks before, he knew nothing about Jesus. He received a mouth organ and a pair of socks for attendance and good conduct. Being still thirsty for the Word of Life, he gave his socks to a boy, who in turn, was to lead him a thirty-minute walk to the South Gate Daily Vacation Bible School.

The second day he did not arrive so the teachers thought it was too much for him, seeing the distance was great and the streets narrow, some places there not even being room for a rickshaw and person to pass, but later they learned that not having anyone to lead him he had started off alone and was knocked down and unconscious by a rickshaw. The next day he arrived, led by his little sister. He still continues to come to Sunday school. Please remember him in prayer.

Philip and Elaine are helping fix a swing in their canary's cage. Philip calls his canary Dickie and Elaine named hers "Cherry". We also have a little kitten added to the family, called Whitey, because of its color. Elaine often tries to sneak a black and white and a yellow kitten into the house but out they go when caught. Philip will be six in October so we expect to send him to the C.I.M. school for missionaries children at Chefoo after the winter holidays which end the last of January. I tried to weigh Keith this morning but as the scales only weigh up to fourteen lbs. I didn't succeed.

There is much food for prayer these days. Let us thank God for travelling mercies and that none of our missionaries have been killed or hurt so far in spite of the hostilities. There has been much seed sowing at Special meetings, Daily Vacation Bible Schools and Short Term Bible Schools please pray for lasting results from these. At Hokow, Mrs. Beard is having a Daily Vacation Bible School for outside children. It is held in the evenings as the people go to the country in the day time since Hokow has been bombed twice. The bus station was hit but not many were killed. Our Superintendent hopes we will be able to go back to Kiangsi this Fall but we have not been told anything as to how long our stay here is to be. We live a day at a time. Please pray for work among the soldiers at Hokow also for blessing on the street preaching there. There is blessing here, classes for inquirers being held twice a week. Quite a few have given in their names as enquirers. I praise God that I was able to complete my required language examinations in April but that doesn't mean I am finished with studying. I would value prayer for help with the language.

Ever Yours,
Florence A. Paulson

XV

Chefoo

Train up a child in the way he should go: and when he is old, he will not depart from it. (Proverbs 22:6)

In the summer of 1940, the family travelled to Chefoo to enrol Philip in the CIM school. Florence was pleased to be able to spend some time there with him and help him adjust, as he was a rather shy, sensitive child. Later she wrote,

> The summer of 1940 we spent in our Mission school. How glad I am we were permitted to have a time at Chefoo and see how well the children are looked after and how happy they all are.

The city of Chefoo is situated some 550 miles north of Shanghai in the northeast part of Shantung Province on a protruding arm of land that points across the Yellow Sea toward Japan. It is a port city, and at the time the harbour was filled with British and American ships. In 1940, it had a population of 200,000 and was home to 1,000 foreigners, served by more than thirty businesses, banks, restaurants, churches, a newspaper office, and an amusement park. White homes covered with red tile roofs dotted the hills overlooking the bay, giving the city a distinctive look.

As part of the Japanese invasion of China, Chefoo was taken in February of 1938. The Chinese authorities hadn't put up any resistance—no fighting, no skirmishes, no loss of life. Japan was at war with China but not with Britain or the United States, so foreigners had little to fear.

The CIM's boarding school, which was situated in Chefoo and established for the education of the missionaries' children, was considered neutral. The school sat on an isolated bay facing the beach and comprised five Victorian-looking buildings. It was a beautiful setting with flowers and trees accentuating expansive lawns. To the east were the fringes of First Beach, and to the west, a backdrop of low Chinese hills.

Initially the school had been established as a convalescence home. In 1879, the founder of the CIM, James Hudson Taylor, who was seriously ill at the time and looking for a place to recuperate, came to Chefoo and bought a bean field from a local Chinese farmer. On the site a convalescence home was constructed from locally quarried stone. Wood, oak beams, and Norwegian pine were obtained from a ship, *The Christian*, which had run aground in the bay. Teak and various furnishings were taken from another wreck, *The Ada*. From there, the Chefoo school was developed, and was officially founded on June 15, 1896.

The school followed the British educational system and focused on excellence in physical sport and academic attainment.[42] The headmaster, Patrick A. Bruce[43] (known as "Pa" Bruce) had played cricket for Cambridge and rugby for Harlequins. Students were taught cricket, soccer, rugby, tennis, gymnastics, rowing, track, and swimming, and were required to take a daily compulsory plunge into the cold waters of Chefoo Bay.

Swimming was taught by the compulsory method. A number of the younger boys would be taken out in a boat captained by the swimming master. Alongside the boat in the water would be several of the older boys. At a designated spot the swimming master would ask the first young boy if he wanted to jump in, dive in, or be thrown in the water. "Usually the victim would say hesitantly, 'I guess I'll jump in, sir.' 'Then jump!' said the instructor. . . . Down into the depths would go the boy, the water becoming murkier as he went. . . . He would take a mouthful or two of salt water, and then, just as he thought his last hour had come, he would rise to the surface, spluttering and half-drowned. . . . A senior boy would grab him by the hair, and tow him to the boat, where he would be hauled up unceremoniously. . . . There he would sit on the edge of the long boat, coughing the water out of his lungs, eyes streaming, and watching the efforts of his fellow victims. . . . A few minutes later the boy's turn would come around again. 'Do you want

---

[42] Because of its excellence, children of foreign diplomats and businessmen also attended the school.
[43] Patrick Bruce was financially independent and never took a salary from the CIM.

to jump in, dive in, or be thrown in?' the master would ask. 'Guess I'll jump in, sir,' would be the probable reply."[44] And thus a swimmer was produced.

Academic subjects at Chefoo included Latin, French, English, history, geography, art, music, and scripture, as well as the maths and sciences. The curriculum, which heavily emphasized classical courses, was designed to prepare students for entrance to British universities, such as Oxford and Cambridge. The teachers were missionaries—most of them were graduates from British universities. Academically, the students took matriculation exams at sixteen years of age for entrance into Oxford University. The exams were sent to England for marking, with Chefoo invariably ranking high in the annual results. A number of the students later became missionaries in China, while others, such as the author and playwright Thornton Wilder, left their mark in other areas of life.

School lessons were rigorous and interspersed with three weekly athletic sessions. Monday, Wednesday, and Friday were designated for serious sports like cross-country running. Every Friday, lessons were interrupted by an amah[45] who entered each classroom and went from child to child, cutting their fingernails. At break time, the children would leave their classes to play rounders, hopscotch, marbles, and hide-and-seek. In their first year, students kept silkworms and learned to wind off the silk from the cocoons. Mail came at meal times and the teacher at the end of the table would assist the youngsters in reading letters from their parents.

Outside of class, housekeepers acting as surrogate parents cared for the children. They would read to them, mend their clothes, and fit them for hand-me-downs. They even taught the children to knit. Amahs made the beds and did the laundry, while Chinese servants did the cooking. The children slept in dormitories. Discipline was quite Victorian and consisted of: washing mouths out with a toothbrush and Lifebuoy soap for telling lies, hitting a wooden pillar with one's bare fists for bullying and aggression, caning, and being gated within the grounds of the school.

Saturdays were activity and sports days. The children would go on treasure hunts, swim in the sea, have picnics in the hills behind the school, or go on walks to various sites such as the Bamboo temple and the monastery. On their

---
[44] Miller, pp. 50–51.
[45] Amahs were Chinese women hired to attend to the personal needs of the children and do general housework.

outings, the children were used to seeing armed Japanese soldiers wearing khaki tunics, knee-length boots, and steel helmets. Some of them had swords dangling from their sides. The Japanese typically were friendly and did not bother the students or school personnel.

Sunday was church. David Michell, a fellow classmate of Philip's, described their Sunday routine in his book, *A Boy's War*. On weekends, the students wore white uniforms consisting of little shirts and shorts that buttoned around the waist. Early Sunday morning they lined up in pairs and wound their way out of the compound in a long line to go to church. They walked along the waterfront and the edge of the Chinese community, through the foreign settlement, past the homes of the Western business community and the interested gaze of the local populace. Then they marched part way up Consulate Hill, en route to either the Union or Anglican church, depending on the affiliation of the student.

In the afternoon, there was an informal church service in the assembly hall—a large meeting area on the compound where the walls were decorated with paintings depicting the story of The Pilgrim's Progress. After the service, the students lined up and went on their regular Sunday walks. The foreign cemetery was a favourite destination. In keeping with the principles of the Sabbath the children were not allowed to run around, though, often, they surreptitiously hid behind the upright gravestones and monuments of some of the missionary pioneers in a game of hide-and-seek. Sunday afternoon was also the time for writing letters home.

XVI

Shangjao

The Lord is my rock, and my fortress, and my deliverer; my God, my strength, in whom I will trust . . . . (Psalm 18:2)

After leaving Philip in Chefoo in September of 1940, the Paulson family travelled to Shanghai for supplies via Darien. In a letter to friends and family, Florence wrote:

> I had my first real taste of sea-sickness between Chefoo and Darien. After two weeks of hurried repacking we left by boat for Kiangsi Province via Wenchow Chekiang. The China coast was blockaded,[46] so it was only by much negotiating that a large party of missionaries got to go inland. We were quite comfortable in the first boat, but when we had to change to a small Portuguese boat at the mouth of the Wenchow River, our excitement began. The boat contained one cabin, the Captain's. Mrs. Smith and I shared it because we both had babies (Keith). The others were packed like sardines on and around a huge pile of luggage. In the wee hours of the morning a search light began to play on our boat then, Boom! Boom! Big naval guns were fired, the shells whizzing just above our heads.
>
> However, we arrived safely at Wenchow and were warmly met by Mrs. Wosley, our C.I.M. hostess while there. We left Wenchow by small boat up river, two couples remaining behind to look after our stores and baggage which hadn't as yet been cleared through customs. A flood came and we had to anchor at a very dangerous place where missionaries

---

[46] Since 1937, Japan had established a naval blockade along the east coast of China. By capturing the seaports and blockading the coast, Japan could control any entrance or assistance to China from the sea. Any foreign boats attempting to navigate the coastal waters were to be destroyed. To frequent these waters meant death for any crew and their passengers. Although Florence frequently talked of the blockade, she always did so with a bit of excitement in her voice and reverence for the God who preserved them.

a few months earlier had been robbed. Three days to wait with very little food and water soaked bedding were no joke, so we turned back only to find the customs premises had been flooded. Also sugar, hymn books, beans, writing paper, etc., had been submerged in three feet of river water. A month later, when our boxes arrived at Hokow, the boatman wondered if they contained wine as dried prunes and sugar made it smell like a brewery. Our groceries had been put in a tin-lined box and not sealed, so the river water got in it and it hadn't been dried out. We were fired on by rifles early one morning while on the river boat, but no damage was done, and after a bus trip and a train trip and another boat journey, we finally arrived at Hokow where we packed up our belongings and moved to Shangjao, our new station for us to work in.

Shangjao, also called Shangrao, is a town on the Kwangsin River in Kiangsi Province. The region was mountainous and the town, which had a population of some 10,000 people, was a major communications centre. People travelling west from Chekiang and Anhwei Provinces had to pass through Shangjao, which was the first big town they encountered on the railway. Kwangsin River was always busy with launched junks.

In the early 1940s, Japan started a bombing campaign in Northern Kiangsi as part of their push west to capture the railway lines. Shangjao was right in their line of fire. The ringing of a large bell warned of an attack.[47] Then, as civilians left the city for the safety of the surrounding hills and countryside, or as refugees crowded the roadways, the planes would commence their strafing, focused on wherever movement was evident.

Unless there was direct danger to the missionary as a foreigner, the CIM expected their missionaries to face the same perils and hardships as the Chinese people. As Hudson Taylor had stated previously, "We are in our stations at God's command, and as His ambassadors, and therefore have both promise of, and claim to, His protection. . . . A holy joy in God is a far better protector than a revolver." (Austen, p. 20)

---

[47] These bells were quite huge, often measuring three feet in diameter, and were struck with a thick rod or paddle.

Florence: A Missionary in China

In January of 1941, Florence wrote her mother.

Shangjao, Kiangsi
January 14, 1941

Dearest Mother:

It is the middle of January. We have invited Mr. and Mrs. Koo to have dinner with us on Friday. They like foreign food. We were invited to a feast on Sat. It was not extra good. One dish was very good but the other dishes had too much red pepper. We took Keith in a bamboo cart which we bought. The children have a great time wheeling each other around in it. We are making bread today. There is a bakeshop on the street but they want 50 cents for very small loaves so it is too expensive to buy bread. The Baptists have opened up work here. Their two Chinese evangelists have arrived. Their wives and children came to services yesterday and came in here afterwards. They are from Shanghai. Elaine is having a great time playing outdoors. Yesterday she and Keith saw a fox chained up. They fed it peanuts and led it around on the chain. Cliff went to Yangkow yesterday, one of our outstations for the morning services. Yesterday we only had 14 at the children's services. In the evening a former school principal, now a lawyer, gave his testimony as to how he came to be saved. We are late having dinner today. Cliff started off for Hokow last week to get the remainder of our belongings but the bus was late coming so he didn't wait for it. He was going to take Elaine with him. Now they will have to go this week. A Christian has repaired his house so he has asked us to have a Christian service in thanksgiving.

We receive letters from Philip regularly. He seems to be happy. Mr. Taylor said he had grown and was looking real well. We had supper with them one night. The Chinese are all busy preparing for their New Year. It is very difficult to buy meat as the tax has been put up to $6.00 a pig. We want to do some hams for winter. We have not had it very cold yet. We have only lit a fire to dress the children by in the morning. Mrs. Cheng and I were out preaching on Friday. We visited three homes and preached to a large crowd by the river.

Keith and Elaine are both very fond of sugar cane so I brought them some home. They chew the cane and get the juice out then spit out the pulp. It is nice and sweet. We had some at the feast Saturday. We have only had one Christmas letter and that from Wimborne from a woman who hasn't written to us all the time we have been in China. Mail is slow but we get it eventually. Men have come with charcoal just as we were eating our dinner. We have had our meat and vegetables but we haven't had our cereal coffee yet. We have oranges for dinner and pudding for supper. Mrs. Koo sent us in some Nanfeng oranges yesterday. They are small loose skinned with practically no seeds and are very sweet. Misses Moody and Wriglet Hay have gone to Hokow to live so we haven't anything to do with regard to managing Hokow affairs. Keith is still asleep. He woke up once but I put him back to sleep.

We have to buy all we need for two weeks because at Chinese New Year there is nothing to be bought. I still have letters to write for knitted clothing given to the children from missionary groups at home which we term "Helping Hands".

I made some cocoanut cookies after dinner but they are not baked yet. Mr. Fu just came in. He is a very nice man. He would like us to go to Yangkow to live. The sun is very warm today. I would like to go out preaching but other things must be done. If Cliff takes Elaine to Hokow she will have to have her sweater washed. It is a good day for drying but alas the day is nearly over. I must close so this can go to the post office along with other letters.

God bless and keep you.
Your loving daughter, Florence

In separate correspondence, Florence detailed the Christian work being done at Shangjao and the outstations.

Schoolboys at Shangjao, Kiangsi
At Hokow the children's work was greatly blessed. The boys from a nearby school came daily to repeat Scripture verses. Every verse learned was printed on colored paper and used to form the link of a chain. Some learned the Lord's Prayer, the Ten Commandments, read a tract, and repeated twenty verses of Scripture. After they had completed a prescribed course they were given a Gospel of John, had a time of games, and were given peanuts as a treat. Some came despite persecution. The parents of one little boy would not allow him to put his verses up in the house, so he kept them in his pocket lest they be destroyed.
—By Mrs. C.T. Paulson[48]

Saved Through A Business Meeting
One rainy Sunday a young veterinary surgeon walked five miles to the China Inland Mission station at Shangjao, Kiangsi, where he found a business session of the church in progress. I slipped out of the meeting to greet him,

---
[48] *China's Millions*, June 1941, p. 86.

and learned that he wished to purchase a Bible. In the guest hall I showed him the various styles of binding we had on hand, and he made a selection, saying that he had read the testimony of the Generalissimo and he too wanted to become a Christian. I explained the Way of Salvation to him, and then and there he accepted Jesus Christ as his Saviour. From that day until he was sent elsewhere he was a regular attendant at services. In a very short time he had read through the Gospels and Genesis, asking many intelligent questions about things he could not understand. He grasped much truth in the few weeks he was in Shangjao, and sought to lead his friends to the Lord.
—By Mrs. C.T. Paulson, Shangjao, Kiangsi[49]

In her final correspondence from Shangjao, Florence talked about the troubling times they faced:

We spent five busy happy months at Shangjao. There were 17 baptisms there in November 1940 and one in January. A veterinary surgeon walked in 15 li and said "Since Generalissimo Chiang is a Christian I want to be one too". He had heard the Generalissimo's testimony. After having the way of salvation explained to him, he accepted Jesus as his own personal Savior. He bought a Bible and came regularly to meetings until he was moved away.

Mrs. Cheng, a refugee woman from Hangchow, was great help in the work. Together we visited Christians, preached in homes and on the streets, led women's meetings and weekly children's meetings. A number of the older girls confessed to have a saving knowledge of our Lord Jesus Christ just the Sunday before everything was broken up by bombings (45 Japanese planes came). Our house was badly damaged. The school and adjacent building leveled with the ground. We had to hire men to shovel the plaster and debris out before we could enter our home. An incendiary bomb fell beside Mr. Paulson's office. It went 12 feet into the ground. Luckily it fused out instead of exploding.

The greatest blow was the death of my beloved fellow worker, Mrs. Cheng. She was hit by shrapnel on the thigh and bled to death before help could come to her rescue. (The soldiers could shoot anyone who moved while the enemy planes were overhead). We barely got outside the city ourselves before the planes arrived and, in the rush, little Keith got taken by a Chinese Christian who was wheeling him in a child's wheelbarrow to the very place where a number of bombs fell. We called them back to stay with us. The Chinese were

---

[49] *China's Millions*, October 1941, p. 155.

afraid the soldiers would shoot them if they moved, but we being foreigners weren't. We proceeded to the gate when outside the city we took shelter in cubby holes dug in the side of a hill. Truly God was merciful in sparing our lives during these two weeks of constant bombing.

Since the Shangjao house was badly damaged we moved 35 li away to an outstation by the name of Yangkow which was formerly a main station because the people in Shangjao refused to rent property to foreigners.

XVII

Mrs. Cheng

Blessed are those who are invited to the wedding feast of the lamb.
(Revelation 19:9)

In the CIM periodical, *China's Millions*[50], Florence gave an account of her friendship and missionary work with a Chinese woman, called Mrs. Cheng.

CHINA'S MILLIONS

By Mrs. C. T. Paulson, of Kiangsi

"OUR HELPER IN CHRIST"

THE TILE-MASONS had come down from the roof, where they had been rearranging the tiles to keep out the rain, and were now lying down in the shade of the building: some were quietly smoking bamboo pipes; others were already asleep. The children had ceased their play, and even the rope-makers, who could be seen through the open gate, had stopped the grinding of their machines, for it was two o'clock on a hot, sultry, June afternoon. All was still, so I particularly noticed the one woman who was abroad at such a time. Round-faced and energetic-looking, she walked through the open door of our guest hall. I knew from her appearance that she was not a local Kiangsi woman, but had come from the neighboring province of Chekiang. Kiangsi women wear trousers, while many of the Chekiang women wear a full black skirt with the usual blue tunic. This was my first meeting with Mrs. Cheng, who was destined to become my faithful friend and fellow-worker.

---

[50] December 1944, pp. 180–182.

Mr. and Mrs. Cheng were illiterate idol worshipers whose original home was in Hankow. Later they moved to Shanghai where they spent their time gambling and feasting. It was in Shanghai that their first son was born and, true to Chinese custom and hoping their family would continue for many generations, they named him Chang-ken, which means "Long Root." Mrs. Cheng contracted tuberculosis and it became necessary to employ two servants, one to do the housework and the other to care for the baby.

From Shanghai, the Cheng family moved to Hangchow where for the first time they heard the gospel. Mrs. Cheng accepted the Lord Jesus Christ as her Saviour. Her life was completely changed: old things were passed away and all things became new. She stopped feasting and gambling and spent her time learning to read the Bible, witnessing to others and praying. The ravages of disease were arrested in answer to prayer and when I met her she looked the picture of health. Two more children were born during their stay in Hangchow and, in keeping with Mrs. Cheng's change of heart, the little ones were given the Bible names of John and Miriam.

Mrs. Cheng continued to grow in grace despite the persecution suffered from her husband, who refused to listen to her pleas for him to repent. He left her for a time and went south, but as Mrs. Cheng was now strong physically she was able to look after herself and her family.

Mr. Cheng returned to his home shortly before they had to flee before the advancing Japanese army. Multitudes fled from the city in terror. In the confusion someone put their baggage on one boat while they were forced to get on another, and thus they lost their possessions. Mr. and Mrs. Cheng took their three children and an older girl, daughter of a Christian neighbor and the wife-to-be of their eldest son.

After weary days of traveling on foot, when many weaker ones fell and died by the roadside, the Cheng family at last arrived safely in the province of Shansi. Sometimes their only shelter had been a disused temple shared with beggars and their food government rice doled out to refugees, but Mrs. Cheng never lost her joy in the Lord. She sought to win other refugees and beggars for Christ. On wet Sundays the family waded through water, carrying their shoes and stockings with them to be put on at the church door. During special meetings Mrs. Cheng was always present, welcoming strangers, quieting an unruly child, urging mere curiosity-seekers to stay and listen to the message or helping a convert to read a newly bought Bible or hymn book. She was an inspiration and a help to all.

After a time spent in the country the family moved to a refugee camp. The Chinese Government provided free rice and shelter and the refugees made straw sandals, wicker baskets, and other items to sell, earning enough money to buy vegetables and clothes. While in camp, Mrs. Cheng led a man and his wife to the Lord. This man came to our Mission later to buy a Bible and I was privileged to help him begin to learn to read.

Sad days befell Mrs. Cheng, for her husband left their corner of the camp and went to live with another woman, who had four daughters. Mrs. Cheng could not endure the jeers of her neighbors so she took her children and future daughter-in-law and moved into the city. The church allowed her to use two rooms on the Mission premises in return for her services as caretaker, and she was entrusted with Gospels for sale. She went from house to house selling the Gospels and witnessing for the Lord Jesus, with the result that eleven persons confessed faith in Him, including her eldest son, Chang-ken. This young man was given work in the post office through the kindness of a Christian official, and his bride-to-be found work in a Christian school.

One of the eleven converts, Mrs. Chang, was the wife of an innkeeper from North China. The first time she came to our Wednesday afternoon women's meeting she carried on her arm a finely woven and beautifully lacquered basket. After the meeting she came to the book room to buy a Bible and gospel posters, the latter to be pasted on the walls of her guest hall. Her purchases completed, she went back to the meeting room to pick up her basket but it was not to be seen and she went home without it. Mrs. Cheng was not satisfied, however, but spent the rest of the afternoon praying and searching, searching and praying, until she found the missing basket. Although it was already dark, and Chinese women do not go out alone at night, she insisted on taking the basket back to Mrs. Chang for fear this new inquirer might be stumbled by the loss.

One bright Saturday morning in early spring, Mrs. Cheng and I set off with a supply of tracts for distribution. We walked down the main street, passed the post office, giving out tracts as we went along, then turned into a narrow, winding street of old China which led us to the new modern road.

We went through the massive city gate where a lone, khaki-clad guard stood watch on the crumbling walls, and crossed the bridge which spanned the moat that separated the old city from the new. The open market stalls lined the bright new road. New stalks of Chinese cabbage, glistening water chestnuts, succulent greens, earthy sweet potatoes, tender bamboo roots, and greasy cakes made of bean flour were temptingly set out for sale. An apron-clad refugee was putting long strings of Chinese noodles into an iron cauldron of boiling water flavored with a little pork, soybean sauce, bean curd and red peppers—an open air restaurant. Smartly dressed military officials walked briskly to and from the bank; handsomely gowned officials' wives sallied past in rickshaws; country grandmothers bumped along on wheelbarrows; haberdashers hawked their wares; and peddlers, carrying portable showcases slung from both ends of stout carrying poles, jostled one another. School boys crowded around and hampered traffic when we began to give out tracts, so we hurried through the city, greeting those marketers whom we knew, until we crossed the new bridge over the river and we were in the country. Along the motor road were occasional straw-covered booths where hot tea and oil cakes were sold to over-burdened, perspiring coolies. Wheelbarrow loads of immense sacks of rice or huge bundles of sugar were left beside the road while the barrow men cooled their aching bodies under the shade of a mat shed, refreshing themselves with delicious green tea. We gave tracts to proprietors and customers alike, speaking a word for our Lord as we did so.

Crossing another bridge we came to a cluster of mud-walled houses with their complement of water buffaloes, pigs and chickens. We asked for the home of Mrs. Tang and were taken through a number of dirt-floor, untidy dwellings to a room in the center of the village. Here an elderly Christian woman greeted us. A young mother sat in a chair with a child of three summers on her lap. The boy's limbs were twitching and his eyes rolling uncontrolled in a high fever. We had heard that this grandchild of Mrs. Tang was dangerously ill and had come to offer what comfort we could. We read from the Bible, prayed, and exhorted the child's mother to put her trust in God, but she sat unmoved. When we left her a little gift to buy something for the child, however, she beamed upon us and loud were her entreaties for us to stay and partake of the noon meal; but we could not stay. The grandmother accompanied us as we began our homeward journey, telling us all her troubles—how her daughter-in-law refused to listen to her; that her husband was dead; and her son, who once attended church, now stayed at home with his wife. In a field beside the road some men were digging up sugar cane which had been buried to preserve it for this year's crop, while others were cutting it in pieces about a foot long, to be planted this spring. We distributed tracts to these men.

Standing in the road we committed our Chinese sister and her household to God in prayer, and she returned to her home while Mrs. Cheng and I headed for the Mission by a short cut. On the way we met a woman who asked us an oft-repeated question: *Would we give her rice to eat if she became a Christian?* We explained to her that Christ died for her sins and that she should first seek the kingdom of God and His righteousness.

By then it was high noon, but we felt led to stop at one more village. I gave a tract to a man selling water chestnuts, who told me he was a Christian. Mrs. Cheng visited a backslider and tried to persuade her to come back to the Lord, but she was not successful.

Next we visited a poor Christian widow whose only son was in the army. She was thinking of marrying her daughter, a bright young Christian, to an unsaved army official. This family had once been prosperous but they were now poor; the mother and daughter were living on a few dollars earned by sewing—and the mother's eyesight is poor—and by keeping safe in their one room the belongings of some soldiers who had gone to the front. Their food was coarse rice and greens, unsavory to a northerner who likes noodles and steamed bread. The proposed marriage seemed to be one way out of their financial distress, so it was not easy to persuade the mother not to marry her believing daughter to a non-Christian.

Early on Sunday afternoon we went out in the highways and byways to invite the children to their regular meeting. We came back with a group of youngsters at our heels and as soon as we entered the chapel we began teaching them choruses. The chapel door being open, others were attracted by the singing, so before the Bible message was given there was a goodly gathering of children, and a few older people. Grandmother Liu sits on the second row from the back; she is a Christian and has brought her little grandchild with the deformed thumb to hear the gospel. The three children of a tall, well-built coolie, who wears his hair done up in a knot like a woman's, we recognize among the group. The oldest, a boy of ten, has baby brother in his arms, and little sister with her hair in pigtails sits by his side. Three or four teen-age girls file in at the back; and we smile and nod our recognition; they are neighbors of Mrs. Chang (the lady who lost her basket) but others come whose faces are new to us.

After Mrs. Cheng has finished teaching the choruses she goes into a little hallway and gets down on her knees to pray while I give the message. My subject is "Salvation." I use the object lesson of the four boxes: First, a black box representing our sinful hearts; then a red box, representing the shed Blood of Jesus Christ. The black box fits inside the red one, illustrating the covering power of the Blood of our Lord. The red box fits into a white one which represents a heart washed white as snow. A black mark is made on the white box but quickly erased to show that if we who have put our trust in Christ confess our sins, He is faithful and just to forgive our sins and cleanse us from all unrighteousness. These all fit into a yellow box which tells of the joy of heaven. God's Word, coupled with prayers and tears, was the means of the salvation of the older girls that day. Thereafter, rain or shine, those girls walked all the way across the new city and into the old each Sunday afternoon to hear the Word of Life. In the meantime Mr. Cheng had returned to his family and he, too, accepted Jesus Christ as his Saviour and attended services regularly. Chang-ken was taken into the army and trained to be a truck driver. The woman who had so wronged Mrs. Cheng came to the city and, in the largeness of her heart, Mrs. Cheng took her and her four daughters into her home and fed them until they could find a home of their own.

About that time we heard air raid warnings almost daily, as our city was the headquarters for the Third Military War Zone, but one Friday in April, 1941, the rapid clanging of the urgent alarm warned us of imminent danger. I hurried out of our house with a Chinese boy who was wheeling our youngest child in a bamboo wheelbarrow; while my husband locked up the house, put our little girl on the handle bars of his bicycle, and started off for the north gate of the city. In the crush of fleeing humanity we became separated. When we were about 150 yards from the gate, the solders cried out for all to hide as the roaring of enemy planes could be heard. The Chinese boy ran for the path into the garden below, taking our baby with him, but when he saw me pushing on in face of the soldiers, who are ordered to shoot anyone who moves while the planes are overhead, he followed after me. One desperate effort and we were all out of the gate, but still had a ravine to cross and a grave-covered hillside to scale before reaching the dugouts, which looked like rabbit holes. We had no sooner ducked our heads under the small clay roofs, some of us crouching in muddy water, than the roar of planes overhead was heard. We could see the twenty-seven planes in relays of nine circle round and round, then heard the *whine* of falling bombs and the *zoom*! of their explosions. The bombing continued about forty minutes, but it seemed like hours. Before going back to the city we climbed the hill to judge, by the ascending smoke, where the bombs had struck. The coolie's son, who attended the children's service, came to me crying: "Our house is hit! Our house is destroyed and I can't find my mother or my baby brother or sister!" We comforted him as best we could but found out later it was not his home but our compound that had been hit. A bomb had fallen just where the Chinese boy and our baby had left the path and sought refuge in the garden. How we thank God that we were able to get out of the city!

We arrived home to find our compound a mass of ruins. The first thing we did was to search for two old Christians who, too feeble to flee, had hid under the bedding. The room next to them was demolished and the tiles of their room had fallen on the bed. They were badly shaken but neither had received a scratch. A goose sitting on eggs in the same room was still in the same position.

The front of our house, the school and teachers' dwellings were gone, and the church and chapel roofs damaged. Back of the school, the evangelists kept pigs: the roof of the sty had fallen and crushed a few of them, but in order that nothing be wasted a man was already preparing one to be eaten. An incendiary bomb had fallen just outside the window of my husband's study and we could not go into the house because it had not exploded. We called the police but as they could not come immediately we stood out among the ruins. We had eaten nothing since early morning and it was seven o'clock in the evening before we could sit down to a meal. The incendiary was fused out the next day.

Friends called with the news that Mrs. Cheng was dead. I could not believe it at first—I thought she might have been wounded, but she could not possibly be dead, because she was so well and happy only the day before. Later I learned that she had gone out of her home under a small tree. She kneeled to pray and was hit with a piece of shrapnel on the thigh and bled to death before the planes left.

Her two sons were called home for the coffining service. Mrs. Chang gave $12 to buy cloth and with the help of a friend made the white gown for Mrs. Cheng's burial. (White is the color of mourning in China.)

The funeral was held at daybreak the following morning. A little company of sorrowing relatives and friends followed the coffin to the graveyard. The woman who had wronged Mrs. Cheng followed, weeping bitterly.

We laid to rest that day a true soldier of the gospel but we rejoice to know that "they that be wise shall shine as the brightness of the firmament; and they that turn many to righteousness as the stars for ever and ever," and that we shall meet again where there shall be no more death, neither sorrow, nor crying.

XVIII

Chefoo Under Advisement

And we know that all things work together for good to them
that love God . . . . (Romans 8:28)

Despite the relatively compatible relations with the Japanese occupants of Chefoo, it was acknowledged that Britain and the United States might enter the war at some future date, and the Mission school considered whether or not they should evacuate. British consular officials in Shanghai pointed out that if such a large section of the community in Chefoo and Shanghai left, there would be panic on the part of the Chinese people. Mission leaders were asked not to organize a mass exodus and were reassured, if they were caught in the midst of war, that the British government would guarantee their prompt rescue. Shortly after Philip's arrival at Chefoo, headmaster Pa Bruce sent this letter[51] out to the missionary parents:

> You are sure to have heard of the advice given by the American consular authorities to their nationals to leave China as soon as possible. British authorities have not sent out any such advice, though it is evident to us that the situation is serious. We in Council have spent many hours discussing the situation in its various aspects, particularly in relation to the Chefoo Schools.
>
> Our General Director, Bishop Houghton, and I went to interview the highest available British Embassy official, and after that, with Mr. Dreyer, went to see an important American consular officer.
>
> Both these authorities concur with our opinion that, in spite of the threatening outlook, our only course of action is to continue to keep the schools open. In any provision for the care of the children, the British authorities have agreed to treat the Schools as a unit, without discrimination of nationality.

---

[51] Michell, p. 20.

M. J. Paulson

This decision to keep the schools open in Chefoo has only been arrived at after fully facing the possibilities that might arise in the event of conflict in the Far East, because we realize the impossibility of moving as a unit to any one of the home countries. The Chefoo Schools have weathered many a storm in the last sixty years, undoubtedly owing to the prayers of parents and scores of others interested the world over, and I believe that this will be the case again. Anyhow, nothing can touch us apart from the permissive will of God, who undoubtedly causes all things to work together for good to those who love Him. This is the fact upon which we now rely.

I understand that a cable is being sent to the home centers telling of this decision to remain open and asking for special prayer for the schools during these critical days.

Yours very sincerely, Pat A. Bruce

For those parents who weren't able to see their children for Christmas, including Florence and Cliff, another letter[52] was sent.

China Inland Mission
Prep School Chefoo
27th December, 1940

Dear Parents of Prepites:[53]

Christmas Day 1940 has just passed, and we who have spent it with your children want to tell you, who must have longed to do so, something of the happenings.

We began the holidays with about fifty Prepites, and, perhaps because we were such a large family, the spirit of Christmas came to us very early.

. . . Just before Christmas the well-known story of Scrooge once again delighted youthful eyes and ears and prepared the way for the Spirit of Christmas 1940. On Christmas Eve little messengers went around the compound or to the houses of other friends carrying bulging bags, waste paper (baskets) or even laundry baskets full of gifts, while others with dolls' prams filled them with gay packages and wheeled them off. Meanwhile a bevy of artists from the Girls' House transformed our dining room into a Christmas bower, where red and green and silver glowed in the soft lights from the tree.

---

[52] Michell, pp. 21–22.
[53] Chefoo school entailed three divisions of students: a boys division, a girls division, and a Preparatory school for elementary students. The elementary students were called "Prepites," ranging from ages six to ten.

Just as supper was over a Chinese school visited us and filled the hall with their hearty singing while our children looked on in solemn amazement. Then, as the last of our excited little family jumped into bed, the corridors were lit by torches, and another bank of carollers gave us the sweet, familiar music that rings in Christmas for us Westerners whether at home or abroad. These were rewarded by [our] donations in a box marked "Relief" which, at the end of the evening held nearly $200.

That night a package found its way on to the foot of each bed, not quite burning a hole through the covers in the few short hours till Christmas Day in the morning. That morning began at 6:30, and instead of the clanging of a gong, church bells relayed by a gramophone echoed down the passages. Breakfast was followed by family prayers round the table, and again the soft lights on the tree shed their radiance over a scene which you would love to have looked upon. Our hearts bowed in worship as we sang of the one who came, "A little Child to earth, long ago" from the knowledge of whom comes all peace and joy and love.

After a short interval we met again in families to open the presents which lay stacked up on floor or tables, and I wish you could have seen how eyes sparkled as books, dolls, aeroplanes, torches (flashlights), penknives or a photograph of you, emerged from their wrappings.

. . . Real families with members in any of the schools, sat together for the service . . . Mr. Clarence Preedy led the service in a Memorial Hall beautifully decorated for the occasion. On the platform was a small Christmas tree with real parcels at its base. These Mr. Preedy opened one by one revealing lettering that reminded us of some of God's gifts to us; beginning, of course, with the Gift of His Son. Dinner of goose, plum pudding, mince pies and all the appropriate accompaniments thereof, was served to nearly 150 people in the Prep diningroom. . . . Each diner was provided with a paper hat, and soon the scene was gay and animated indeed. . . . Mr. Bruce . . . voiced our thanks to all who had helped to prepare the meal, and to the friend in England who had given so generously towards it.

At 5:00 p.m. we all made our way to the Memorial Hall for the final thrill of the day. The platform had been transformed into a well. A curtain mysteriously draped one stairway leading to it, while the centre was lit by fairy lights. At once the whisper went round, "Father Christmas (Santa Claus) is going to come out of the well." At length . . . Father Christmas himself appeared, a dignified figure in spite of his somewhat small and unsteady conveyance. Once on the platform, he found no difficulty in making the well produce suitable gifts for all. At last came the gifts for all the girls and boys; a well-filled stocking for those of Prepite age and something more useful or enduring for those of riper years. His work well and nobly done, Father Christmas was wheeled out of the Hall followed by admiring and affectionate glances, and tired but contented little people made their way home to supper and bed.

. . . Let us together thank the Great Giver of every good and perfect gift, whose loving-kindness alone made such a world at such a time as this.

XIX

Yangkow

To everything there is a season, and a time to every purpose under the heaven: A time to be born . . . a time to plant . . . a time to laugh . . . and a time to dance . . . . (Ecclesiastes 3:1–4)

Because of the heavy Japanese bombing of Shangjao and the loss of the mission home, the family moved to Yankow.

In July, 1941 Florence wrote her mother:

Yangkow, Kiangsi
July 3, 1941

Dearest Mother:

Mr. T'ang just came and brought us some nice new beans. Elaine keeps after me to write to you to get her and Keith each a real telephone with a man in it. She wants a red one and Keith a blue one. I try to explain to her how a telephone works but she still insists there is a man in it. Cliff went to Shanghai yesterday to see Mr. Tuckey. I expect him back to-day or to-morrow. It is hot to-day but a breeze makes it not unbearably so. Keith is washing and Elaine is making Chinese shoes. Miss Barham sent us four books to read. A person needs reading material during the summer as it is too hot to go out very much and the days are long. Mr Lui just came to borrow the paper. We haven't had any foreign papers for a few weeks now. We had floods twice last week but the water did not come into our compound. It washed a t'ing-tsi away. A t'ing-tsi is a shelter in a park or along the roadside where one can rest during a journey or find shelter in time of storm. The children are playing in a tub of water. It is cold, just out of the well. Water keeps them busy for quite awhile. Keith can talk quite a bit now. Just got a letter from Philip this morning. He won two ribbons at the prep sports. Mr. Taylor said he was looking happy and well. I don't expect we will go away this summer. This house is quite comfortable. There is not much fun with children in a house full of people, four in a room. The first watermelon is in the market so we will stay home and enjoy watermelon. Elaine is very fond of it but Keith doesn't like it very much. Peaches and plums are very plentiful just now. Young chickens are very expensive. I had one for my birthday otherwise we haven't indulged in such a luxury. We had roast duck and dressing last week. It certainly tasted good. Things spoil so quickly that liver and pork are about the only meat one can buy because they are eaten up at one meal. It is almost dinner time. I don't know where the morning has gone. Bread goes moldy very quickly in this weather so we have to make it more often. My wadded jacket was green with mold so I had to sponge it off and sun it. I wonder how the war between Russia and Germany will come out and what will Japan do? We are anxious to know. I must close now. Re the telephones. They can wait until we get furlough. We haven't applied for it yet but hope to soon.

God bless and keep you,
Your loving daughter
Florence

In another piece of correspondence, Florence wrote,

We spent a happy year at Yangkow and, on December 29th, 1942, our 3rd son Blakely Conrad was born. Miss Van Viebahn came from Nanchang to act as nurse and Miss Euphenia Wilson came from Iyang to help in the home. Dr. was killed in a bombing raid.

In May we had Pastor Yin, who was then the Shangjao pastor, come for a month's special evangelist meetings. He is a good worker with a pastor's heart in caring for the flock. He gathered in all the backsliders first. Some had not come to church for two years then he got others interested. One business man said "I want to buy the best Bible you have."

XX

Chefoo Under Japanese Control

. . . I will not fail thee, nor forsake thee. (Joshua 1:5)

By 1941, Japan was tightening its hold on the territory it occupied in China. More restrictions were implemented all the time, and Westerners were becoming more isolated. Movement was limited and permission for foreigners to travel across the borders into Free China was difficult to secure. Due to these restrictions, Florence decided to educate Elaine at home instead of sending her to school.

In December of 1941, when Japan attacked the American fleet at Pearl Harbor and declared war on the United States, Chefoo school was no longer considered neutral but rather the property of the Imperial Japanese Army. Soldiers marched in and took possession of all the school radios, and demanded lists of school and personal property, down to even the cutlery. Pa Bruce, the headmaster, was arrested and imprisoned at the Astor House Hotel, along with five Western businessmen from the community. The *Kempeitai*, the Japanese equivalent of the German Gestapo, interrogated him as if he were a spy regarding the route he had taken through Siberia on his last furlough to England, despite it being a common route for travellers.

A notice was affixed to the high metal double leaf school gates establishing the compound as Japanese property, and guards holding rifles and extended bayonets were posted at the front entrance. Young boys from the Japanese school, which was built adjacent to the Mission school, hurled insults and rocks over the stone walls. Japanese officers took possession of the foreigners' houses and cars in the city.

The school authorities again discussed the possibility of relocating to Free China or to some other country. South Africa was bandied about as a possibility. However, they did not feel it was safe or practical to evacuate such a large group of children. Thus, the decision was made to remain in Chefoo.

A more urgent matter was the question of funding. With the declaration of war, they could obtain no funds from the Mission's headquarters in Shanghai. Consequently, a harsh budget was worked out that, if adhered to, would mean the school could survive another four and a half months with the funds on hand. Food would be rationed. The adults and older students would receive only five slices of bread a day, Chinese staff in the school would be drastically reduced, and chores such as sweeping, cleaning and setting the tables, and dishwashing would be done by the older students. Studies were reduced in order for students to pick up additional housekeeping duties. Rationing was, however, aggravated by off-duty Japanese guards, who would regularly walk into the kitchen and help themselves to food. This pilfering continued until one of the missionaries put up a notice in Chinese that read, "We have had no instructions from the Japanese authorities to feed Japanese soldiers," after which the plundering stopped.

Pa Bruce was permitted to leave prison for Christmas Day as a goodwill gesture, but confined again afterwards. The school continued to pray for him: "How long, O Lord? Remember, O Lord, what the measure of life is. Remember, O Lord, how Thy servant is scorned."

> Because he cleaves to me in
> love, I will deliver him;
> I will protect him because he knows my name.
> When he calls to me, I will answer him;
> I will be with him in troubles,
> I will rescue him and honour . . . him.[54]

Pa Bruce was finally released a month later, on January 25, 1942.

Later, an order ensued that all the senior girls were to be recruited as prostitutes[55] for use by the Japanese Navy. Pa Bruce emphatically refused the demand. Nonetheless, everyone was now required to carry identity cards and wear a white armband whenever they left the compound. The armband, which was four inches wide, was stamped with a black letter designating the

---

[54] Miller, p. 138.
[55] The Japanese authorities customarily provided brothels comprised of enemy women for their military. The Japanese called these women "public toilets."

country of origin: "B" for British, "A" for American, "N" for Norwegian, and "X" for everyone else. When the teachers or Japanese soldiers were not looking, the American students would have some fun by turning the "A" on their arm band upside down, chalking out the cross bar and proudly wearing a "V."

The situation at the school was fast becoming both complicated and frustrating. Former Chinese servants started selling information about the school and staff. Japanese soldiers held bayonet practice in the sports field. Members of the Japanese military regularly came to take measurements of the classrooms and dormitories while reassuring the staff that the school would never have to leave the compound. Chinese burglars would try and break in at night, and Japanese soldiers, wounded and bleeding from battles in the hills with Chinese guerrillas, would arrive at the school in need of care.

Communication with the school—when it existed at all—was extremely limited. All letters written in English were confiscated and declared property of the Japanese government. The only mail that arrived were letters written in Chinese on thin rice paper and enclosed in Chinese-style envelopes. Later it was discovered that letters written in English, as long as they were enclosed in Chinese-addressed envelopes, would also be delivered.

One letter, written by a staff member, outlined the difficulties of the times:

Feb. 9, 1942

The following extract is from a personal letter just received from one of the staff at Chefoo, and knowing the difficulties of the times, I thought it good to send it on to you in case you might be feeling some anxiety about the children.

"It must be weeks since you heard of the children, for no mails are allowed in or out these days. . . .

We have cut down our meat and milk bills by half and dismissed a number of servants. The boys and girls in the other schools set the tables and clean rooms. Here the staff do their chores and spread bread. It is quite a business to clean your room before school in the mornings. We are also limited in the number of pieces of bread that we eat; the Preps eat nine a day. At supper they are allowed one every five minutes and each is very particular that no one gets over his share. We are having the most interesting meals, tou-fu (bean curd) in a large loaf for dinner.

Of course we see no fruit, though we have a lot of vegetables and often have raw cabbage and carrots for a salad. I am sure that no one has talked so much about food for years. We spend absolutely no money outside the compound more than is absolutely necessary. We are ripping up war knitting, scarves, etc., and making them into cardigans for the children. The staff are busy knitting stockings and other necessities.

I wish that I could tell you of the wonderful way that God led certain people to prepare for this contingency. Others outside the compound were fearful of changing money at a low exchange and were left with almost nil and a small stock of coal, whereas the head of affairs in the compound had laid in a stock of coal for the winter, and it was wonderfully sent in when there seemed none to be had. Also Mr. Jackson had been extraordinarily wise, you can guess along what line. Then at Christmas, our puddings had been made weeks beforehand when supplies were not short and Mr. Oleson very nobly killed one of his goats to supply most of the compound with Christmas fare.

Then as for presents! We could almost write a book on the way the Preps were able to have about five little parcels each. Just the day or so before things closed up a large parcel post came in from Shanghai bringing quite a store of children's presents from parents down there. An evacuating mother left a veritable toyshop behind with Miss Carr, and the toys were all as good as new. Two large parcels for a little boy in Kansu had been lying with us for a year or two, and we took the liberty of disposing of its contents. Another evacuating child left us with ten tins of jam. Another parcel from America with gifts of books came too late for last Christmas and came in handy this one. It was marvelous.

Then we have been so glad to hold our Memorial Hall services so that we could all meet together on Christmas morning. In the afternoon we had games as usual and then the Boys' School put on a very good puppet show, which was followed by Father Christmas coming down the chimney. He came with cholera certificates and the usual passes and enormous photos of himself. Mr. Bruce and most of the inmates of Astor House were allowed home for Christmas and had to report again next morning at 9:00 a.m." (Michell, pp. 28–29)

As time wore on, more soldiers were posted to guard the school and no one was allowed to leave the compound. Food was further rationed and the children began to lose weight. Only heavy doses of cod liver oil prevented serious malnutrition. Japanese soldiers roamed throughout the compound. Eventually the school's funds were completely depleted. Turning to God, the staff and students met for a special evening of prayer to ask for God's guidance and provision. Later that evening, some Chinese Christians, at great peril to themselves, threw several sacks of peanuts over the wall. Inside one of the sacks was six hundred dollars in Chinese currency. Although the school was under Japanese rule, it was definitely in God's hands!

Slowly, the Japanese started taking over the school premises. By the end of August 1942, they had taken possession of the hospital, the doctors' residence, and a block of staff residences. Next they took possession of the Prepite school building, and Philip and his classmates had to move in with the older boys, classrooms having been sacrificed to make new living quarters. By November 1942, the entire fifteen-acre site and all its buildings had been expropriated. Finally, orders came that the school had five days to move—all two hundred children, as well as teachers and staff.

Florence, by this time, had not seen Philip for two years and was uncertain of his circumstances. She stated, in a letter to her CIM supporters and prayer partners, her friends, and her mother:

> How dear you all are to our hearts in these very trying days. Glory is to God, who changeth not, and we have abundantly proved his faithfulness these two years, a shade by day, a covering at night; food in the wilderness; strength in time of weakness; courage in time of danger, a protection from evil men and a comfort in sorrow. . . .
>
> Alas, the last we heard is that the Japanese have taken over the schools and that the first party of children was to leave Chefoo, Sept. 19, and a second boatload three weeks later. The children were being taken to Shanghai. Whether they are there and the schools allowed to re-open, we do not know, or whether they have gone to South Africa or elsewhere we do not know.

Florence: A Missionary in China

Florence Annie Bradley, age 16

Florence and Clifford's wedding picture, Calgary, February 7, 1931

M. J. Paulson

Florence and Clifford's prayer card given to supporters when leaving for China, 1934

"This is our party on the boat going to China. Cliff, myself and Philip, Kester, Kalbitz and Smail. Front row: Hill, Cronhielm and Carlson". –Florence

Florence: A Missionary in China

Clifford, Philip and
Mr. Bareis,
Hwaining, 1935

CIM headquarters
in Shanghai

Top left: Ascent to Kuling, 1935

Top right: "Just coming up over the mountains into Kuling"
–Clifford

Main street in Kuling

Florence: A Missionary in China

Florence with Philip

Bottom left: Philip

Bottom right: Philip and Chinese friends

Philip and Elaine

Philip, Clifford, Florence, Elaine and baby Keith, Shanghai, 1939

Florence: A Missionary in China

Florence, Clifford, Keith, Elaine and Philip wearing his school uniform, Chefoo

Keith

M. J. Paulson

Elaine, Florence, Clifford, Blake and Keith on the family's return to Canada

Back row: Keith, Elaine, Philip
Middle row: Blake, Clifford, Florence
Front row: Duane, Lucille, Marguerite 1952

Florence: A Missionary in China

Marguerite and Florence,
Peking, 1987

M. J. Paulson

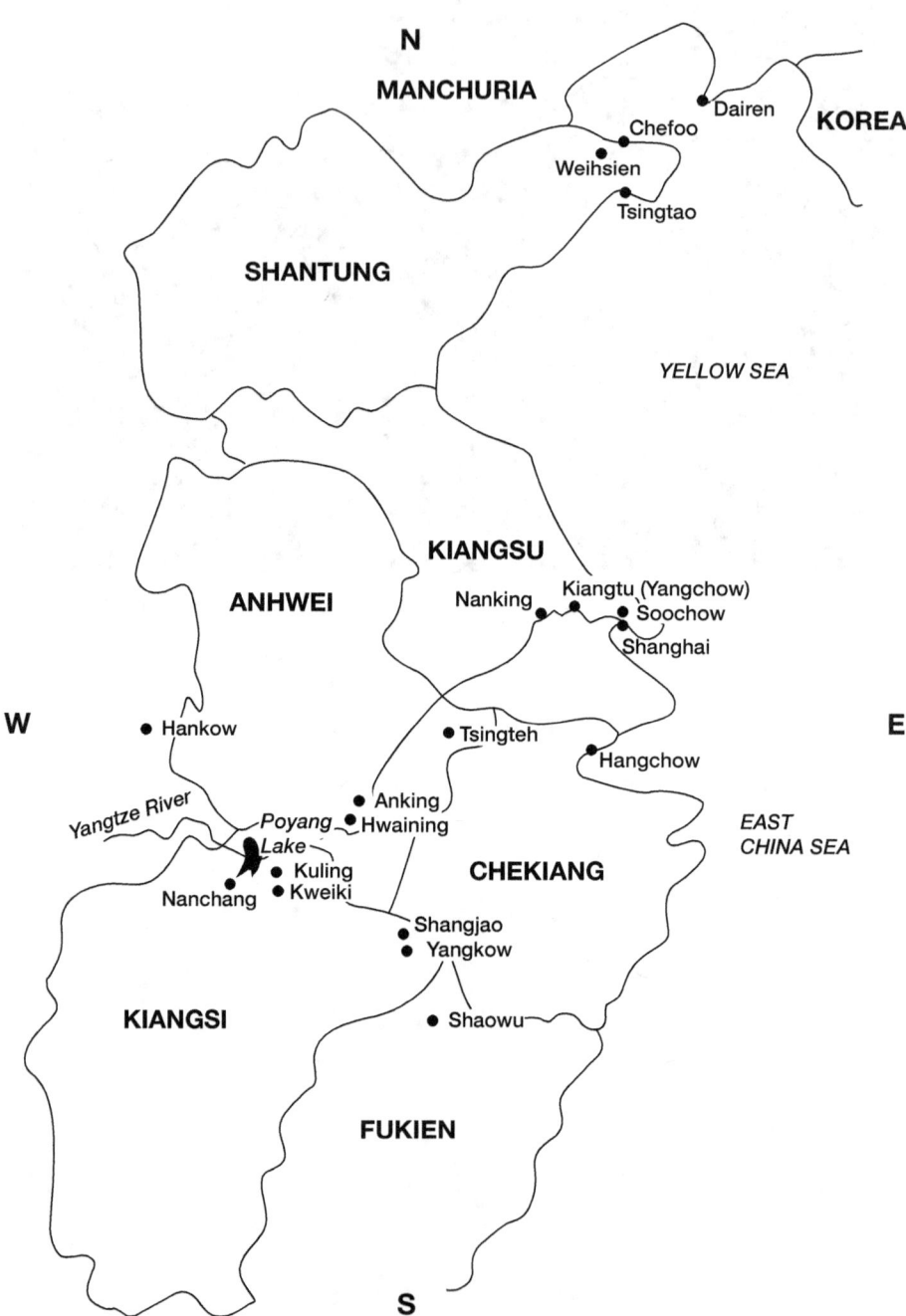

Map of the Chinese provinces and locations where Florence and Clifford worked and travelled during their time in China

Florence: A Missionary in China

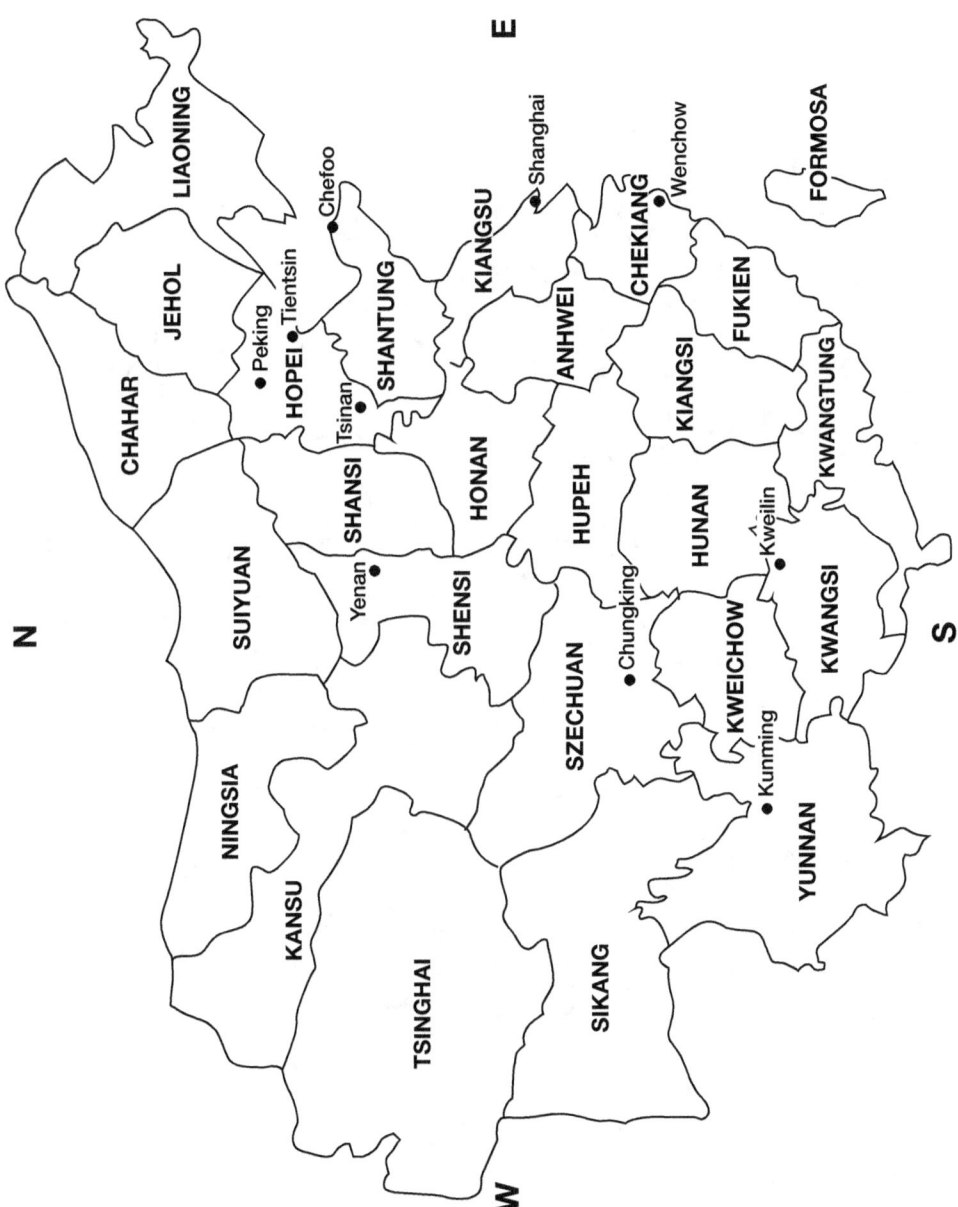

Map of China 1930

M. J. Paulson

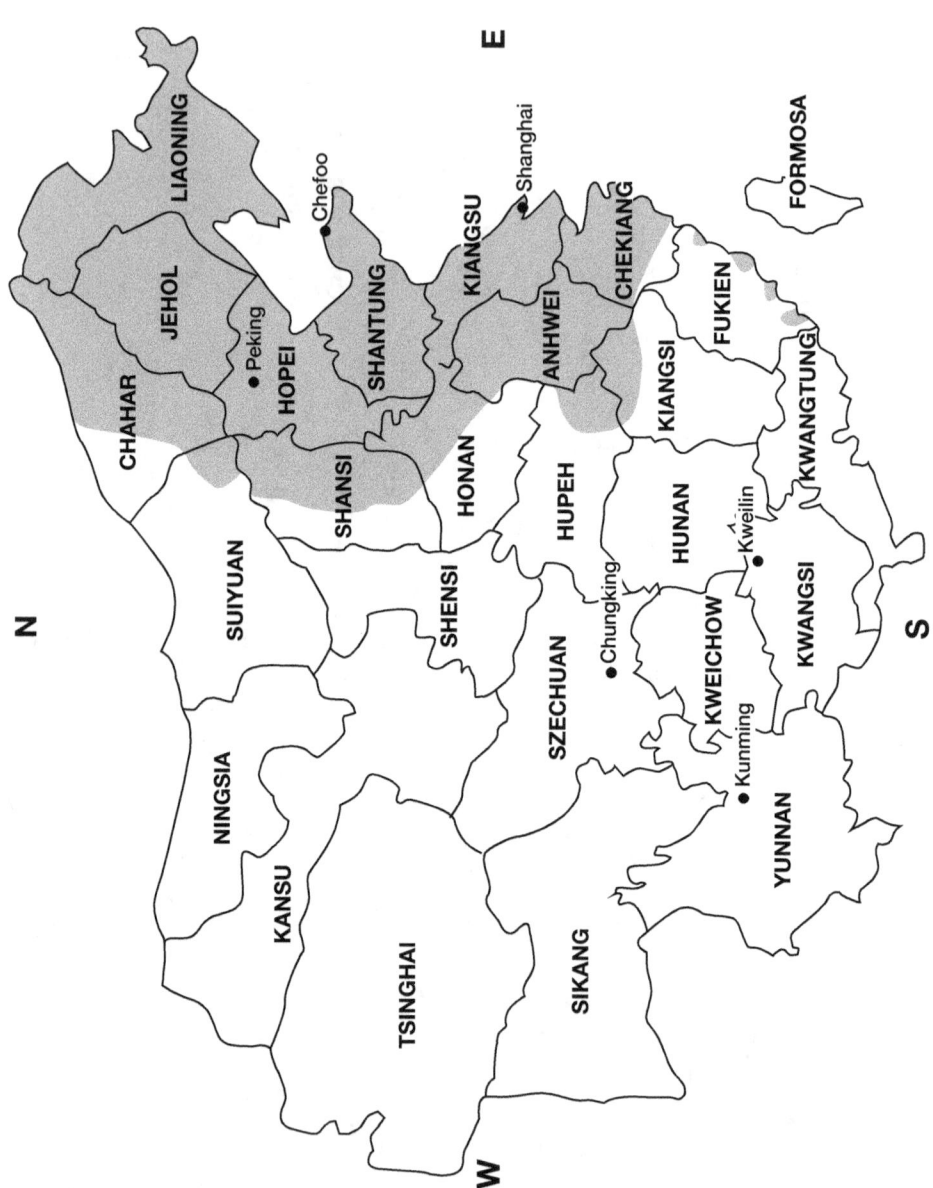

Map of Japanese occupied territories in China (denoted by the grey area) in the 1930's and 40's

XXI

Doolittle Raid

Crossing the Bar[56]
BY ALFRED, LORD TENNYSON

Sunset and evening star,
    And one clear call for me!
And may there be no moaning of the bar,
    When I put out to sea,

But such a tide as moving seems asleep,
    Too full for sound and foam,
When that which drew from out the boundless deep
    Turns again home.

Twilight and evening bell,
    And after that the dark!
And may there be no sadness of farewell,
    When I embark;

For tho from out our bourne of Time and Place
    The flood may bear me far,
I hope to see my Pilot face to face
    When I have crost the bar.

On April 18, 1942, the United States of America launched a surprise bombing attack on the home islands of Japan. It was four months after Pearl Harbor and the United States' official entry into WWII. After Pearl Harbor and America's demoralizing defeats in the Pacific, the raid was intended to bolster American

---

[56] www.sparknotes.com/poetry/tennyson/section10.

morale and attack Japan's sense of invincibility by demonstrating that Japan was vulnerable to American air attack.

The plan was devised in secrecy and included having a number of medium bombers launched from a Navy aircraft carrier within striking distance of Japan. The planes were to fly over Japan, bomb various military and industrial targets, and then fly on to China for refuelling. Several makeshift landing strips were to be prepared near the coast of China, in Chekiang Province, and homing beacons were to be used to guide the pilots in. The planes were to land and refuel before continuing on to Chungking in Szechuan Province, the wartime capital of Chiang Kai-shek and the Kuomintang government.

Several problems needed to be worked out for the plan to succeed. First, the planes, B-25 Mitchell bombers, had to be modified to reduce their weight and consequent fuel consumption. The planes needed to carry a bomb load of ten tons. To lighten the planes and accommodate other equipment, various items had to be removed including the lower gun turret and the liaison radio set. The planes also needed to carry as much fuel as possible because of the distance to be travelled: a total of 2,750 miles. Consequently, additional fuel tanks had to be installed. Even then, there would only be enough fuel for the flight. Launching bombers from a carrier had never been done before because the take-off distance was so short. For weeks on end, the pilots had to practice taking off at short distances. Although they eventually became proficient at short take-offs, they would not be able to return to the aircraft carrier as the runway, which proved sufficient for take-off, was not long enough for landing. After bombing Japan, the planes would have to continue westward and refuel in China.

In all, sixteen bombers would be used in the attack. Each bomber had a five-man crew, including a pilot, co-pilot, navigator, bombardier, and gunner, all under the leadership of Lieutenant Colonel James "Jimmy" Doolittle. The mission would be called the "Doolittle Raid," and the men Doolittle Raiders.

At 0738 on the morning of April 18th, the American aircraft carrier the *U.S.S. Hornet* and its cargo of bombers were sighted by a Japanese patrol boat, which then radioed an attack warning to Japan. As a result, the decision was made to launch the attack earlier than planned. Initially the carrier was to get within four hundred miles of Japan and the bombers were supposed to take off just before dark, bomb at night, and then proceed to China, arriving after daylight early the next morning. Now they had to be launched immediately, the planes having to fly longer—200 miles more than what was planned to reach Japan. Although the pilots had practiced short take-offs on land, they had never before taken off from a carrier and the 476 feet of take-off distance was extremely short for their needs. Unbeknownst to them, the Japanese patrol boat's warning was not taken particularly seriously, as it was not believed that an American vessel could get that strategically close to Japan.

The bombers quickly departed, all sixteen of them, at five-minute intervals, the first at 0820 and the last at 0919. They flew in groups of two to four before changing to single file at wave-top level, just fifteen to twenty feet above the ocean, to save on fuel and to avoid detection and anti-aircraft fire. Around noon, six hours after launch, the planes began arriving over Japan. Flying as low as the terrain would permit, just over the tops of trees and houses and through valleys lower than the hills on either side, each aircraft found its separate bombing targets. Then, for the actual attack, the planes climbed to 1500 feet, lest the explosives destroy their own planes, and dropped their five hundred-pound bombs.

After the bombing, the scattered aircraft proceeded southwest along the southern coast of Japan and across the East China Sea toward eastern China and the makeshift airstrips supposedly awaiting them. In case the aircraft did not make it to land, the pilots were to set the planes down in the water and take rubber boats to shore. The flight was perilous. Somewhere over the China Sea, between Japan and China, the airplanes encountered rain and stormy weather. Night was approaching and the aircraft were running low on fuel, which was further depleted as they flew through thick squalls, bucking the storm. As they proceeded into the night, the weather deteriorated further: the coastal areas of China were overcast and shrouded in mist and fog. Visibility was zero. None of the planes would have even reached China had it not been for a fortuitous twenty-five mph tail wind that increased their ground speed for seven hours over the last 1,200 miles of the trip. Jacob Manch, co-pilot for one of the planes spoke of their ordeal: "It was about this time that the Good Lord started giving us a hand . . . the wind shifted and gave us a tail wind, all the way into China. This is contrary to the winds in that country as they should have been flowing in our nose, from west to east. If we had not received this tail wind for about seven hours, we figured we would have landed about 200 miles out in the China Sea, out of fuel." (Glines, p. 156)

Of the sixteen aircraft, twelve of them, after fourteen hours and 2,200 miles of nonstop flying, finally reached the Chinese coast; however, they were unable to find the airstrips. The night was dark, with thick fog and rain, and the terrain was unfamiliar. Unbeknownst to them, the Chinese were not prepared for their landing and the airstrips were unmanned: there were no lights, beacons, or landing flares—only total darkness. Although Chiang Kai-shek had been informed that the United States needed several airfields on the Chinese coast for the landing of American planes, for purposes of secrecy he had not been informed of the actual raid on Japan. Nor had he been told by personnel involved with the raid to have the fields ready, even though Doolittle had arranged with Admiral Halsey to send Chiang a coded message to that effect. For whatever reason, the message was never sent.

Despite the state of the airfields most of the planes might still have landed safely, had Chennault, the leader of a group of volunteer American air pilots reporting directly to Madame Chiang Kai-shek, been informed. With notification, he could have established radio contact with the bombers and assisted them in landing. But because of poor American communication and guarded decisions, fifteen of the planes crashed: twelve crews bailed out and their planes crashed in the mountains when they ran out of fuel, and three of the aircraft crashed in the ocean not far from shore. Another flew to Russia shortly after leaving Japan, as it was the closer land mass and the plane was already dangerously low on fuel.

Despite the disastrous circumstances there were only three immediate casualties. Crew number six, named for the order in which the planes left the aircraft carrier, ran out of fuel and crash landed four miles off shore in the East China Sea, along the coast of occupied China. Two of the men, bombardier William Dieter and engineer gunner Donald Fitzmaurice, were severely injured on impact. As the plane was sinking, the rest of the crew climbed atop the wreckage and pulled Dieter and Fitzmaurice with them, until they were all swept away by huge waves. Robert Meder, the co-pilot, grabbed Fitzmaurice by his life jacket and swam to shore only to discover that he had already died. Dieter was able to swim part of the way but succumbed to his injuries and was washed ashore by the tide. The only other casualty besides Dieter and Fitzmaurice was engineer gunner Leland Faktor from crew number three, who died when, upon landing, he parachuted into the mountain and fell down a cliff. The Japanese captured eight other crewmen, three of whom were executed—the remaining five were imprisoned. Robert Meder was one of the captured men, but he died in the prison camp from dysentery and beri-beri. One of the other prisoners, Jacob DeShazer, went to Japan as a missionary after his release from captivity at the end of the war.

The Japanese military, out of humiliation and anger, set out to find the crews of any of the American bombers who might have come down in Japanese-controlled territory. The troops searched Kiangsi and Chekiang Provinces for the Americans for three months, covering hundreds of square miles. Worried that the Americans could launch further air attacks from the sea and refuel in China, or even fly bombers directly from China, all airfields within 20,000 square miles of the coast of China were ripped up.

Of the sixteen planes, Doolittle's was the first to leave the aircraft carrier. After dropping his bombs on a factory in Japan, he flew west, reaching the coast of China after dark. By 0930 fuel was low and he was unable to find the airfields in the heavy fog, so he ordered his crew to bail out and crashed his B-25 on a nearby mountainside. He was seventy miles north of Chuchow, near Tein Mu Shen. He jumped from 6,200 feet and landed in a rice paddy that had been freshly fertilized with human excrement and recently ploughed. He remained close by for the night. The next day he found a Chinese military detachment and, eventually, the rest of his crew. From there, they walked and rode in sedan chairs, and then travelled by riverboat heading toward Chuchow. While hiding in the cabin of the riverboat they were approached by John Birch, a young American Baptist missionary.

Birch had arrived in China in 1939 and was stationed at Hangchow, a city of 200,000 people about 100 miles south of Shanghai. He preached in the area and made several excursions into Shangjao, where he met the Paulson family. On April 27th he was:

> at a crowded Chinese inn in a small village on the river. He sat down at a rough wooden table and ordered a cheap meal of boiled red rice, green bamboo shoots and a meat scrap. A moment later a Chinese man came and sat down silently across from him. "You American?" he whispered.
>
> John sensed a need for secrecy in the man's voice. Without looking up from his meal, he gave a barely perceptible nod.
>
> "You finish. Follow me." The man took a drink, then a few more bites before adding, "Be very careful. Enemy eyes may be watching."

Nothing more was said. John ate slowly, allowing the Chinese to finish first. Then after he left, John paid for his meal and walked out casually. At the door he saw the man starting down the path beside the river. Shouldering his pack, John followed him.

The man came to a halt by a small enclosed sampan river boat that lay low in the water, obviously heavily loaded. The stranger jumped aboard and motioned to John to do the same. After looking all around to assure himself no one was watching, John followed feeling more curious than frightened. The nervous little man John had been following rolled his eyes toward the door of the boat and announced mysteriously, "Americans!"

Americans? John thought incredulously. Americans out here? It couldn't be. If there were any Americans within a hundred miles I would know about it. They must be missionaries trying to escape from some place. What is going on?

He walked over to the door and knocked softly. "Are any Americans in there?" he asked in his soft Georgia drawl.

Silence. Then a muffled voice saying, "No Japanese could make up an accent like that!" The door swung open and John entered the dark hold. He blinked a moment, adjusting his eyes to the faint light given off by a lantern that swung from the low ceiling. Then he shook his head, finding it hard to believe what he saw: five overgrown American flyers stuffed into the little hold, all grinning at him.

"Wha—what? Who? How?" he stammered.

The commanding officer gave him a little mock salute and introduced himself. "Colonel James H. Doolittle, United States Army Air Force." (Hefley, pp. 84–85)

Birch accompanied Doolittle and his men part of the way to Chuchow, acting as their interpreter and liaison as well as arranging a military escort the rest of the way to Chungking.

On his way to Chuchow, Doolittle located and met with Cliff. Doolittle gave him $2,000 in Chinese currency that he had brought with him from the States. Initially the money was intended for the ransom of the captured American airmen, but when that enterprise proved fruitless, Doolittle decided to use the money for burial costs of his dead airmen. He instructed Cliff to give the $2,000 to John Birch to buy a plot of land for the burial of Faktor from crew number three. By then, Birch had returned to Shangjao where he received a telegram from the American Military Mission in Chungking ordering him to report to the nearest air base at Ch'u Hsien.[57] While there, he found two more crews of Doolittle's men and was assisting them in a flight to Chungking when "a phone call came from a Canadian missionary friend, Reverend C.T. Paulson, at the town of Yangkow. 'Doolittle was just here on his way to Chungking and left some money and special instructions for you,' Paulson informed him. 'How soon can you come?'" On April 30th, "the next day the Canadian missionary handed him the $2,000 in Chinese money left by Colonel Doolittle with his orders: 'You are to bury Corporal Leland D. Faktor and any others who may be brought in for burial, arrange medical aid for any injured, obtain all information possible on missing aviators, serve as secretary/translator to aviators stopping over at Ch'u Hsien, accompany the last crew to Chungking, and report to the Military Mission there.'" (Hefley, pp. 89–90)

Not only did missionaries provide assistance to the Doolittle Raiders, so too did scores of Chinese people, and at great personal peril. They hid the Americans, fed them, helped them navigate the countryside, and escorted them on their journey to Chungking. One example of the Chinese people's kindness was recounted by Ted Lawson in his book, *Thirty Seconds Over Tokyo*, so named because the actual bombing of Japan took thirty seconds. Crew number fifteen had landed in the ocean. After swimming to shore, a distance of about a half a mile, the men "wandered around in the dark and discovered a goat pen. They started to sleep there for the night, but, after awhile, the Chinese who owned the pen came out, led them to his house, woke up his wife and kids and let the crew sleep in the house. The Chinese family slept in the goat pen." (p. 143)

At this time, the Paulsons, after having their home bombed by the Japanese in Shangjao, had gone to Yangkow—the mountainous area where the American planes had crashed. It was in Yangkow that Cliff met with Colonel Doolittle and later gave the colonel's instructions to John Birch.

After crew number six had crashed in the ocean, the bodies of Fitzmaurice and Dieter, who had been left on the beach, were removed by the Chinese. Two wooden boxes were prepared as coffins for them. The Chinese Christians approached Cliff and asked that he perform a Christian burial service for

---

[57] Also known as Chuchow.

the two Americans. To protect themselves and their families from Japanese reprisal, fearing that the Japanese would find the bodies and desecrate them, they kept the burial a secret. The Chinese Christians led Cliff from his home in the middle of the night through the mountainous terrain. He was blindfolded for his own protection, to keep him from knowing the exact burial site. The Chinese men carried the coffins. The path was narrow and treacherous as the men, in silence, trudged upwards. Cliff was apprehensive. He knew the potential costs: if they were discovered it would mean a torturous death for all, including the villagers and families below. But he was propelled by his faith in God and prepared for whatever might happen. The small procession stopped at a discrete clearing. The graves, which had been dug earlier in the day, were ready to receive the men. The Chinese Christians removed Cliff's blindfold and there, on the mountainside, they buried Fitzmaurice and Dieter. Cliff said a short prayer for the young men and their families, and quoted several verses of scripture. Possibly he even quoted a favourite poem of his, which he had also copied in calligraphy and sent home to his mother in Canada upon the death of his younger brother, Stewart: "Crossing the Bar," by Alfred, Lord Tennyson.

Cliff did not speak of the burial until long after the war, the secrecy of the mission having been emphasized by Colonel Doolittle. Nor did the American government release the full details of the raid for a year afterwards, out of concern for Japanese reprisal against the Chinese people and the missionaries who had assisted the men.

John Birch buried Faktor from crew number three. Birch had attempted to buy a burial plot for him with the monies provided by Colonel Doolittle, but the Chinese military commander at Ch'u Hsien, where Faktor's body had been taken, refused and insisted on donating the burial plot as well as the coffin and headstone. On May 5th, Birch conducted a funeral service for Faktor in an air raid shelter, even though the grave and stone were not ready because of daily air raids. Two weeks later an actual graveside service was conducted with the Chinese Air Force providing full military honours.

True to form, the Japanese military began a campaign of terror in the Chinese countryside, to punish anyone who might have assisted the American airmen. Any Chinese person, who may have helped the Doolittle men or who lived in the villages the men had passed through, were systematically eliminated. Details abound of the atrocities committed: "At Ihwang in Kiangsi

Province, the Japanese found the man who had given shelter to Lieutenant Harold F. Watson. They wrapped him in blankets, poured kerosene on him and forced his wife to set him afire. At this village they also threw hundreds of people alive into deep wells, destroyed American mission property in the vicinity and desecrated the graves in a missionary cemetery" (Hefley, p. 90). Entire villages and cities were wiped out, such as Ying Tan, simply because the Catholic mission there, operated by Father William J. Glynn, had assisted crew number thirteen.

Chiang Kai-shek "was furious at the Japanese onslaught and reported in a cable to the United States Government: 'After they had been caught unawares by the falling of American bombs on Tokyo, Japanese troops attacked the coastal areas of China where many of the American flyers had landed. These Japanese troops slaughtered every man, woman and child in those areas—let me repeat—these Japanese troops slaughtered every man, woman and child in those areas'" (Glines, p. 318). In all, an estimated 250,000 Chinese civilians were massacred by the Japanese army in their search for the downed bomber crews and in retaliation for any assistance provided to them.

XXII

Flight from Yangkow

From coldness to the burning woe,
    Mine eyes have seen, my heart must know;
From weakness in the awful fight
    Against the demons of the night;
From all that would dishonour Thee,
    Christ, my Lord, deliver me.

From fearful calls to do and dare,
    From insincerity in prayer,
From dread of battle—wound and scar
    From seeing mire instead of star;
From all that would dishonour Thee,
    Christ, my Lord, deliver me.[58]

Since Japan's attack on Pearl Harbor, any American, British, or Canadian citizen captured by the Japanese became a prisoner of war. As Japan crouched on the doorstep of Yangkow, Florence, Cliff, and their young family were forced to flee to Shaowu, Fukien Province. Always stoical and never one to dramatize, Florence talked about their ordeal in a general letter dated November 2, 1942.

> After an afternoon meeting a military friend came, brought us a little butter and told us Kinhua has fallen, then we knew the war was upon us. Chekiang missionaries were escaping with only what they themselves could carry, roads crowded with refugees, bombers unloading their deadly bombs all around us. A big gun was placed in front of our house. We hurriedly gathered together our clothing, bedding and a few cooking utensils, boarded a boat and went to Hokow. The flood had washed out bridges and planes were just behind us,

---

[58] A poem found amongst Florence's "important papers," after her death.

but we arrived safely at Hokow to find the two lady missionaries living there packing to leave. Mr. Porteous joined us there, having ridden on a train load of bombs. It looked as if we would have to walk from Hokow, as there was the sound of big guns near at hand, with only what we could carry in our hands, but God wonderfully provided 7 wheelbarrows between the 8 of us. After walking 70 li over flooded land, sometimes ankle deep in water with nothing but rice gruel to buy for food at exorbitant prices, we arrived at an outstation in the hills. We lived there for two weeks with very little to buy for food and, at one time a snake, 6 feet long crawling on the tile roof above our heads at night. Thankfully, the snake which had gone to higher ground because of the floods crawled down off the roof and the Chinese killed it. There we were joined by Misses Agnes Baxter, Margaret McQueen, Bessie Huntermore, Olive Finney, Minna Alwarden and Euphemia Wilson.

Since we were in the front with the enemy just over a range of hills and we didn't have any means of getting money, we moved on to where there was telegraphic and postal communications. We walked, but hired coolies to carry the luggage and the three children in two baskets.[59] The children were fine on the trip. God kept clouds over the July sun so although sunburnt we did not suffer too much from the heat. We drank ice cold spring water and being overheated from walking over hills, two of us got stomach upset but not bad enough to cause any delay. There being no suitable premises at Kwangtseh, the last Kiangsi city we came to, we moved on into the province of Fukien to Shaowu where the American Board Mission work was and where the Fukien Christian University is at present situated.

On our journey we let Mr. Porteous be our treasurer and gave him our money. He liked to swim and, passing a stream, he decided to have a dip. He had put our money in his sox for safe keeping. Forgetting it was there, he pulled off his sox and part of our money was carried away by the stream. He scrambled after it and retrieved most of it. We grumbled one day when he saw some nice cakes in a shop window and bought some. Having so little money we thought it should only be used for necessary staple food. On the whole we all got along in the best of Christian brotherhood.

We were kindly received by the foreign and Chinese friends here (at Shaowu) given a house to live in, beds, tables, cooking utensils, etc., to use. The others gradually returned to Kiangsi as the Japanese evacuated that part of Kiangsi

---

[59] Because the coolies were afraid to travel far, Cliff would have to travel back with them to their place of origin, then travel back to Florence, hire another set of coolies to carry the children a few more miles, and then repeat the whole process over and over again.

along Kwangsin River where our stations were the end of August 1942. We stayed on at Shaowu, having been loaned to A.B. Mission for 6 months as Mr. and Mrs. Starrs were leaving for U.S.A. for medical treatment. Our Kiangsi churches had greatly suffered during the Japanese Invasion, Yukan, Ingt'an, Iyang, Yuishan premises were all burned. Shangjao house has not suffered more than the previous bombing. Yangkow has had slight damage. Every station has been looted, so everyone of us has lost part of our worldly goods. We are real pilgrims now carrying our possessions with us.

Please pray for our work here and as to where we will go when we leave here. We will be the only foreigners doing evangelistical work among the local people here. The others will be doing the institutional work. There are between 800 and 900 students here so there are great opportunities. I work in the women's work at the South and East Gate Churches. There is to be a special work done among the students by a visiting preacher.

May God bless and keep you all in these difficult days. With our hand in His we need not fear. Elaine can't go to school so I am going to teach her this winter. Keith had dysentery and malaria this fall but is well and gaining weight now. Baby Blakely is learning to walk. He is fat and very active. Cliff and I both had malaria, but malaria is a disease in which you are very ill while the fever lasts but one recovers their strength quickly because you can eat when the fever leaves. Thank you for your prayers and support. We know when you are praying then God works in answer to your prayers and we see results.

Yours affectionately,
Florence Paulson

In a postscript to the letter, Florence wrote a brief note to her mother:

Dearest Mother,

I have written this because I could only use one sheet of paper.[60] We are safe and well despite dangers as you will realize by reading this. We pray for you daily. God is ever faithful and nothing can happen to us except He allows it. Send out love to all the family. Wish we could send and receive letters.

Yours with much love, your daughter Florence

---

[60] In using every space on her piece of paper, Florence wrote in the margins and vertically up the side of the paper.

XXIII

Temple Hill

God is still on the Throne, and He will remember his own.[61]

On November 5, 1942, the Chefoo Mission School closed for good. The children had packed their belongings—their own bedding, chamber pot and wash basin, and a trunk or suitcase with their clothes and the rest of their personal belongings. The staff had done likewise, but also had to pack medicinal and living supplies, kitchen utensils, school supplies, and books in large trunks or boxes. At the last minute the teachers had given the students permission to help themselves to anything they wanted from the staff lounge. Quickly the students stuffed their pockets with all the luxuries a teacher's staff room could offer including old keys, coins, marbles, and chalk.

Early in the morning of November 5th, the children and teachers were herded outside past the guards. As one of the teachers, Evelyn Davey, walked out, a young student noticed a tiny paw appear over the edge of a basket Miss Davey was carrying. Whispers quickly spread: "'Miss Davey's smuggled out her cat!' With a mischievous wink at the children Miss Davey tucked away the paw and walked demurely past the guards who noticed nothing" (Greenough, pp. 21–22). Together with the cat, all of the girls, the female teachers, three older boys who were helping, and the older retired staff were put in rickshaws, which were waiting outside the compound gate. When the rickshaws left, the remaining group, which included Philip, loaded their belongings onto an old truck and lined up in pairs to walk to their new home. Their destination was the former American Presbyterian Mission compound at Temple Hill, about three miles across the city to the west of Chefoo. The business community

---

[61] Hymn, words, and music written by Mrs. F.W. Suffield.

had already moved there to a large house on the compound. In total, the compound would contain some four hundred prisoners.

Then the boys, in a long line, marched out of the school grounds carrying their own bedding. They passed mounted troops and guards in olive green uniforms shouting orders at them. Against the background noise of clanging swords and rifle butts being stomped on the ground, Stanley Houghton, one of their teachers, led the boys in singing as they walked up the road.

> God is still on the throne, and He will remember His own.
> Though trials may press us and burdens distress us, He never will leave us alone.
> God is still on the throne, and He will remember His own.
> His promise is true, He will not forget you, God is still on the throne.

The long procession wound its way slowly to Temple Hill. Crowds of Chinese lined the street and stared in astonishment while Chinese and Japanese looters rushed into the vacated premises.

Temple Hill was surrounded by a stone wall that was topped with barbed wire and guarded by Japanese soldiers brandishing bayonets. Inside the compound were a church, a hospital, teaching units, and several large detached family houses that had previously been occupied—and trashed—by the Japanese army. Over the back wall and up the hill was the beautiful old temple of Yu Hwang, the Jade Emperor, which gave the area its name. A six hundred-year-old pomegranate tree sat in the inner courtyard.

Philip and the other young boys occupied one of the foreign-styled houses, along with their female school teachers and eight of the older boys to help with the heavy work. The house, with its eight rooms, held a total of seventy-two people. The older boys and their staff occupied the second house—a total of fifty-eight people. A number of older missionaries who'd retired in China and lived at the school occupied the third house, along with another eight boys to help with the work. Behind the three main houses were a number of smaller dwellings: former servants' quarters, a woodshed, a building for laundry, and a garage. The three houses and smaller outbuildings comprised one section of the compound. Another section housed the female students, and a third the Chefoo business community.

Upon arrival the students and staff set to cleaning out the rooms and setting their bedding down on the floor. Their luggage was later brought by truck, and was transported into the houses and set up against the walls in various rooms. Boxes of supplies had to be unpacked, sorted, and placed where accessible for use. Everything had to be organized and made ready for living, an orderly routine established as quickly as possible.

Everyone had to help and had regular chores. There was cleaning and sweeping of floors, cooking, cutting wood, and shovelling coal, and when the coal ran out, there were coal balls to be made out of coal dust and clay. Laundry had to be done, millet ground, potatoes and vegetables peeled, garbage emptied, water hauled, and food bought. Initially, the Japanese did not provide for the compound. Meat was scarce and what could be obtained was often only the entrails of unknown animals. Once, the staff bought some piglets to fatten up and later eat. When the time came for slaughtering them, one of the teachers had to read to the students in a very loud voice in order to drown out the dying shrieks of their pets. Typical fare was most often bean curd, coarse millet bread, and cabbage.

The houses were hard to heat and usually there was only enough fuel for the stoves to heat just one room of the house. Because the children's clothes were wearing out or being outgrown, "new" dresses and shirts had to be made from curtain material. Water for washing was limited and each child only got a little bit of water in his or her own basin for personal bathing, and then everyone would rinse in a common tub. The outside toilets consisted of a hole in the ground near the brick wall in full public view with only a tiled awning above. With the crowded conditions, lack of heating and sanitation, and inadequate diet, illnesses ravished the compound—Hepatitis A, fevers, and dysentery. Roll call was taken every morning and evening with everyone required to line up and call out their number in Japanese. A teacher wrote out the numbers on a large blackboard and placed them where the students could read them at roll call, but not the officer in charge. Of course, the officer was immensely pleased, thinking that the children could count in Japanese and had learned so quickly.

Despite the hardships, the children still pursued their lessons sitting on boxes and trunks lined against the walls of a room that also served as living room, dining room, and bedroom. In the evenings there were concerts or readings put on by the staff members and older students. Midway through their internment at Temple Hill, military authorities turned over control of the camp to the Japanese Consular police. The new commandant, Major Kosaka, allowed sand to be brought in for the children to play in and even let them have a supply of firecrackers for their celebration when festivities occurred at the temple. The commandant, believed to be Christian, kept an English New Testament in his pocket, which he often showed to the internees when his men were not looking.

In an attempt to secure information about his nephew, Philip, Alick Harper, Florence's brother-in-law, wrote the CIM headquarters and received this reply.

E. A. BROWNLEE, B.A., B.TH.
Secretary-Treasurer
for Canada

China Inland Mission
150 St. George Street
TORONTO 5, CANADA

REV. ROBERT HALL GLOVER, M.D., F.R.G.S.
Home Director for North America,
Philadelphia, Pa.

REV. ISAAC PAGE, D.D.
Prayer Union Secretary for
North America

June 24th, 1943

Mr. Alick Harper,
1211 5th Ave. South,
Lethbridge, Alta.

Dear Mr. Harper:

I beg leave to thank you for your communication of June 15th which reached my hand yesterday. It is quite true, as you have learned from your wife's sister, Mrs. Clifford Paulson, that their eldest son is now interned by the Japanese, along with all the rest of our Chefoo school children, the teaching staff, and other members of our Mission in Chefoo, in the American Presbyterian Mission compound on Temple Hill in the outskirts of the city of Chefoo, in Shantung Province, North China. The Japanese authorities have taken over our China Inland Mission compound in that city and are using it for their own purposes. They have also dispossessed the American Presbyterian missionaries at Temple Hill and have interned all our people in various houses on the Presbyterian compound. This action was taken some 6 months ago.

On the face of it this news seems rather serious, and it must be admitted it is none too cheering. We are glad to say, however, that we have received numerous reports from members of our Mission located in Chefoo, written since the time of their internment on Temple Hill, and all of them speak cheerfully and hopefully of their present circumstances and of the future. They are living in rather crowded accommodation, but seem to be getting along fairly well in their limited quarters. Only a minimum of school work is possible, and yet an attempt is being made to keep up classes with the children. All reports indicate that they are securing sufficient food, and are fairly well provided for in the matter of clothing. They also had coal for the cold weather last winter, and taking it all in all, they are full of praise to God for His gracious provision for and care of them under the difficult conditions.

We are not surprised that at time of writing Mrs. Paulson had not heard from her son since sometime last year for all regular mails to and from all points in Occupied China have been mostly irregular, if not cut off altogether. Our latest information, however, is to the effect that brief letters are now being permitted to pass by the Japanese authorities between our C.I.M. children in Chefoo and their parents in Free China. Furthermore, our C.I.M. provisional headquarters in Chungking, Free China, keeps as closely in touch as possible with those in charge of C.I.M. affairs in Chefoo and in turn passes on all available information about the children to their parents in Free China. We feel quite sure therefore though Mrs. Paulson may not have received letters direct from her son, she will nevertheless be fairly assured of his wellbeing and comfort in spite of the fact that he, with all the rest, is interned.

You could, if you chose, make further inquiry through the National Red Cross, but I doubt if you could secure in that way any more specific information than that we have outlined above.

Our C.I.M. group in Chefoo consists of from 150 to 175 school children and some 50 to 60 adults, these last being in part members of the school staff and in part people who were responsible for other branches of our C.I.M. work in Chefoo. Among these are both medical doctors and trained nurses. Furthermore we have been assured that the Japanese have made arrangements for the hospitalization of any of our people who may fall ill. We have the assurance therefore that the health of our entire group is being safeguarded. In this connection we are grateful to be able to say that so far as we know there were no serious cases of illness among our Chefoo people during the last winter season, nor have there been any epidemics of any kind.

There has been considerable talk from time to time of the possible repatriation of some or all of our folk in Chefoo, including both children and adults. Thus far, however, no arrangement so far as we know has been completed for such repatriation, though we understand such a move is still under consideration. Such action, of course, if undertaken, would be through arrangement made by the Japanese Government on the one hand and by the Governments of the United States and Great Britain on the other.

Expressing our sympathy with you in the above-mentioned conditions, which are equally distressing to the relatives of our missionaries and to ourselves, and with kindest greeting, I remain,

       In His service,
       Very truly yours,

             E.A.Brownlee
EAB:B   Secretary-Treasurer

XXIV

Kunming

But they that wait upon the Lord shall renew their strength; they shall mount up with wings as eagles; they shall run, and not be weary; and they shall walk, and not faint. (Isaiah 40:31)

In 1943, Florence, Cliff, and their three small children prepared to leave Shaowu in Fukien Province for their journey out of China. Florence packed their belongings in several carrying cases and left them on the second-floor veranda overnight, in preparation to leave early in the morning. During the night, thieves stole what few belongings they had. Now they would be travelling even lighter than before, with only the clothes on their backs and a few remaining items that they carried by hand. It was a sorrowful departure as they were leaving Philip behind in Japanese hands, not knowing where he was or how he was doing.

From Shaowu, they headed to Kweilin in Kwangsi Province, six hundred miles away. Travelling for the small family was dangerous as the war raged around them; there were armed guerrillas in the countryside and continual bombing and strafing by the Japanese. Diving to about two hundred feet the Japanese would drop their bombs, which immediately exploded upon impact. The explosions sent sprays of steel several feet into the air and extending for about one hundred feet around the bomb site. Most people, however, were not actually killed by the bombs but by being hit with shrapnel and bleeding to death. Those who ran from the bombs were machine gunned by other planes. Numerous times the family was subjected to machine gun fire.

Florence ran through the gunfire with two-year-old Blake, while Clifford pedalled seven-year-old Elaine and four-year-old Keith on an old bicycle. By God's grace they managed to escape any injury, more fortunate than the dead and dying along roads and in ditches that flowed ceaselessly with blood. All told, their flight from China would take four and a half months. To add to their ordeal, the small family travelled alone. "Medicine kits, clothing and food were stolen by starving Chinese along the route. Only because all members of the family were able to speak Chinese were they able to find their way and to obtain assistance as they travelled."[62] Once they found shelter at a Catholic Mission, but the only place to sleep was on coffins already occupied by the dead. Despite these hardships, the family pressed onward. West and north they went, finally arriving in Kweilin.

Moving on from Kweilin, the family travelled by bus another four hundred miles to Kunming in Yunnan Province. Kunming is an old walled Chinese city built on a 6,000-foot plateau and founded in 765 AD. Its streets were narrow and cobbled. It sits on the Chinese side of the Himalayas and is surrounded by mountains to the north, west, and east. Marco Polo, the thirteenth-century Italian traveller, had visited Kunming and wrote about his fascination with its sites. Much later, French settlers arrived, having constructed a railway up from Indo-China to Kunming. They built villas amongst the mud-walled hovels of the local Chinese. Mountain tribes people in faded blue turbans could be seen on the streets having travelled over narrow mountain trails driving pack mule caravans[63] loaded with salt, tin, and opium. Water buffalo, cattle, and pigs frequented the thoroughfares. In summer, the fields were filled with the stark white blossoms of opium poppies.

During WWII, Kunming was an important Chinese military centre, prepared as a government headquarters in case the government at Chungking fell. It was also used as an American air base and transport terminus. After Japan took control of the eastern seaports in China, Kunming was the only means of getting supplies and armaments into the country and distributed to Chinese armies in the field. It was China's lifeline to the outside world, the only remaining link between Free China and the rest of the world. There were two supply and travel routes into and out of Kunming, one by land and one by air: the Burma Road, and the air flight over the Himalayas—called the Hump.

The Burma Road was a major engineering feat. More than 200,000 coolies—men, women, and children—built the Chinese part of the road in 1937 and

---

[62] Quoted in the *Calgary Herald*, April 12, 1944.
[63] In addition to coolies, donkeys or mules were the primary "beasts of burden." Often the donkey's nostrils would be slit so that they could breathe more rapidly under their heavy loads.

1938. Estimates of lives lost during the construction were two coolies for every six feet of road. The coolies worked with picks and shovels, and sometimes even their bare hands, hauling dirt and rock in baskets hung from a pole across their shoulders. Foreign engineers had estimated it would take ten years to complete the road, but it was done in less than two. The road followed old elephant trails, winding along mountain ridges with elevations up to 9,500 feet, across raging mountain streams, and through deep gorges and steep ravines. Two major rivers had to be crossed, the Mekong and the Salween.

Supplies came in from Rangoon, a southern port city in Burma, and were transported to Lashio in north Burma. From Lashio the Burma Road began—717 miles of dirt highway that wound northeast from Lashio through rough mountain terrain toward the Salween gorge. There, it mounted the crest of the gorge and then descended down the sheer water-worn bank in thirty-five hairpin curves, hewn by hand out of solid rock. It took twenty miles of serpentine road to traverse the vertical mile from the crest of the gorge to the suspension bridge that spanned the turbulent reddish-brown waters of the Salween River. On the east bank, the road repeated its tortuous winding up the rocky cliff to the Paoshan Plateau and on to Kunming. In monsoon season the road was un-driveable.

Driving the Burma Road was as perilous as flying over the Himalayas, which was at the time referred to as the "Skyway to Hell."[64] Flights were always difficult and treacherous as the planes had to climb over the 23,000-foot snow-covered peaks of the mountains, constantly combating violent storms, air currents strong enough to break up a plane, bitter cold, and vicious downdrafts that tossed them about mercilessly. The planes were unheated, frigidly cold, and unpressurized, and pilots had to use oxygen tanks and masks for the journey. Then there were strafing and aerial attacks by the Japanese, in an attempt to curtail supplies coming into China.

The airfield at Kunming was out beyond the rice and poppy fields, between the city and a string of lakes. Thousands of coolies had carved the strip out of the raw red clay of that area, which they then covered with broken rocks. The runways were sturdy and could accommodate the heaviest bombers and transport planes delivering supplies via the Hump route from Burma and India.

---

[64] *The Generalissimo*, p. 397.

Besides some Chinese military personnel, Kunming was headquarters for a small group of American mercenary pilots recruited in the United States prior to the attack on Pearl Harbor and led by a retired Air Force officer, Claire Lee Chennault. Although the pilots were officially designated the American Volunteer Group (AVG), they became known as the Flying Tigers. Their insignia was a winged tiger flying through a large V for victory, and the noses of their planes were painted with a shark's head and teeth. Chennault reported directly to Madame Chiang Kai-shek, who had taken over the leadership of the Aeronautical Commission in order to reorganize the Chinese Air Force. Chennault's job was to train the Chinese and American pilots in tactical warfare against the Japanese. Later, Chennault was given other responsibilities: provide air support of Chinese military operations and engage in attacks on the Japanese; protect the Burma Road from Japanese air attack, including the port city of Rangoon and the aerial supply route over the Hump; and defend Chungking and Kunming from Japanese bombing campaigns.

Since being in China, Chennault had obtained captured Japanese pilot manuals that were then translated into English by the Chinese. By studying the manuals, he was able to learn that the Japanese pilots were drilled for hundreds of hours in flying precise formations and rehearsing set tactics for each combat situation they might encounter. As such, they were superb technical pilots and had the fortitude for combat, but likely lacked initiative and judgement, and would tend to go into battle with a set tactical plan and follow it no matter what happened. Bombers would hold their formation, maintaining a constant speed of 160 mph and an altitude of 11,000 feet until all were shot down, and then fighters would engage in the same tactic over and over. In dealing with the Japanese, Chennault sought to have American pilots break up the Japanese formations by bringing a style of fighting for which the Japanese had not prepared. American pilots were taught to fly above the enemy, then dive, shoot, and break away quickly, with the same sequence repeated again and again.

Chennault also observed when the Japanese pilots would break off an attack and start heading for home, they were usually low on fuel and ammunition. If chased, they would either have to turn and fight with limited ammunition or try and manoeuvre, or open full throttle to speed home, running out of fuel and crashing before they made it back to base. Chennault's techniques were novel for the American pilots, who had been educated in tail-chasing dogfights—which was the European style of warfare at the time, but proved suicidal against the Japanese. Chennault's ingenuity even extended to having decoy planes made out of bamboo on the runways to make the Japanese think that the Americans had more fire power than they did.

Chennault's record was unsurpassed in the annals of World War II. "In three years of operations (his pilots had only) lost 500 planes from all combat causes, while destroying 2,600 enemy planes and probably incapacitating 1,500 more; had sunk and damaged 2,230,000 tons of enemy merchant shipping, 44 naval vessels, and 13,000 river boats under 100 tons; killed 66,700 enemy troops and knocked out 573 bridges." (Chennault, p. 354)

In March 1942 Rangoon fell to the Japanese, who then proceeded north to Lashio and the Burma Road, going as far as the Salween gorge. There they were stopped by the Chinese armies, with the Japanese on one side of the gorge and the Chinese on the other. This stalemate lasted well into 1942. With the Burma Road lost, the only route out of China for the Paulson family was by air, flying over the Hump. However, it too was perilous, with many planes not making it and Japanese fighter planes prowling the area and attacking at will.

At Kunming, the family boarded an army plane for the eight-hour, 923-mile flight to Calcutta. The plane had to fly at 23,000 feet to clear the Hump of the Himalayas. The plane was unheated and bitterly cold, although certainly not matching the temperature outside. Vicious downdrafts tossed the plane around, jerking the passengers about despite being strapped into their seats along the ribs of the aircraft and making them sick. Oxygen tanks and masks had to be used at the highest altitudes until the oxygen ran out and the passenger slipped into unconsciousness. Of course, parachutes were not a necessity because the flight path over the snow-covered, treacherous Himalayan mountains meant certain death should anyone be forced to bail out of the airplane, even with a parachute. At one point on the journey, according to then four-year-old Keith, a Japanese plane shot at them, its bullets ripping into the side of their plane.

The plane eventually landed safely in Calcutta, which had been abandoned by the Allies in mid-March 1942. In the Bay of Bengal, the Japanese Navy cruised the waters and made Calcutta untenable as a seaport, despite it being a flight destination from Kunming. The family was safe but destitute. They did not speak the language, had no local currency with which to buy food, and had only a few items of clothing. Fortuitously, the Mission had sent

Mr. R.E. Thompson to Calcutta some time earlier to secure accommodations for evacuating missionaries and to assist with any required paperwork. As such, the family was met at the plane and taken to lodgings, fed, and given a small amount of local currency with which to make necessary purchases.

Elaine, as adept as many children her age, quickly learned the language and would translate from Hindi into Chinese or English when accompanying Cliff to the markets. There she once saw a man squatting on the ground coaxing a cobra out of a basket. As the king cobra slowly weaved its way out, the snake charmer opened a second basket containing his prized Indian grey mongoose. Almost instantly the fight began. Within a few minutes the mongoose dispensed of the cobra, though for most of the struggle all that could be seen was the top of his tail sticking out from the snake coiled around him. Another time Elaine was able to ride an elephant and visit the Taj Mahal. For Christmas, the family sat cross-legged on the ground and ate curry on a banana leaf as their celebratory dinner.

From Calcutta, the family travelled by train to Bombay. Bombay, at the time the largest city in India, was heavily overcrowded. It was situated on an island that was connected to the mainland by several bridges. Cliff, who frequently wrote to world leaders or sent editorial letters to national newspapers on spiritual and political matters, met with Mahatma Gandhi[65] during Ghandi's confinement at Aga Khan's palace near Bombay. The topic of their discussion remains unknown.

After spending some time in Bombay, the family boarded an American warship for a circuitous journey back to Canada. Because it was wartime, all the windows in the boat were covered with black curtains that had to be tightly secured at night. To avoid detection from enemy attack, the ship had to traverse a criss-cross pattern across the ocean. Their first port of call was Australia, where Cliff left the boat for a day. Florence and the children were not allowed to leave—an arrangement made to prevent people from staying in the country illegally. Next, was Los Angeles, the actual point of destination where the family disembarked and made their way to Vancouver by train. It was February 1944.

---

[65] Mahatma Gandhi was a religious leader who sought independence for India from British rule through nonviolent resistance. Although a Hindu, he saw all religions as a pathway to heaven and, in talking about his beliefs, said, "I am a Christian and a Hindu and a Moslem and a Jew." One American missionary described him as "one of the most Christlike men in history (who) was not called a Christian at all." (Fischer, p. 130)

Florence: A Missionary in China

On April 12, 1944, the following article appeared in *The Calgary Herald*.

Missionary Safe Home But Japs Hold Son

Rev. Clifford T. Paulson and Mrs. Paulson and their three children are happy to be back in Canada after nine-and-a-half years in China, including a four-and-a-half month flight before the Japanese, but their happiness will not be complete until 10-year-old Phillip, the oldest child is released from Japanese internment.

Phillip who was born in Innisfail, has been a prisoner of the Japanese for three-and-a-half years. When his parents last heard of him, through the Swiss government eight months ago, he was reported well.

SEEKING HELP

"Now that we're back we are doing our utmost to have the government work for Phillip's release," Mr. Paulson told The Herald today. "We tried everything before leaving China and India but to no avail: perhaps now that we are home the Canadian government will be able to help us."

Phillip was taken prisoner while attending school in Shantung province, China, several hundred miles from his parents' mission in Kiangsi province. The Japanese advance into China was moving so quickly at that time that Mr. and Mrs. Paulson were unable to do anything to rescue their son. They didn't know he was in danger until the town had fallen.

As it was, Mr. and Mrs. Paulson consider themselves fortunate to have escaped

with their three other children—Blake, two; Keith, four; and Elaine, seven.

The family's home in Kiangsi was bombed by the Japs and when they began their tortuous trek which was to eventually take them to India and to the United States aboard an American warship, the parents had to carry the three children in baskets.

TRAVELLED ALONE

"We were machine-gunned along the way and at times we were only a mile ahead of the Jap army," Mr. Paulson recalled.

To make matters worse, the Paulsons travelled alone. Medicine kits, clothing and food were stolen by starving Chinese along the route. Only because all members of the family were able to speak Chinese were they able to find their way and to obtain assistance as they travelled.

The Paulsons finally reached a Chinese town near the Burma border. They managed to obtain accommodation on a plane which flew over the scene of current fighting on the India-Burma frontier and were landed at an Indian port.

TAKING TREATMENT

Mrs. Paulson, with the baby, Blake, still is in Victoria recovering from malaria. Mr. Paulson is in Calgary also taking treatment. With him are Elaine and Keith and all three are guests of Mr. and Mrs. P. E. Jensen, 130 7th Ave. N.W.

Mrs. Paulson is the former Florence Bradley of Stettler.

Mr. Paulson was born in Bawlf. He was educated at Cadogan, Provost, Camrose, where he graduated from the normal school, and at the Three Hills Bible School. He held a pastorate in Wimborne before leaving for China in 1934.

XXV

Departure from Temple Hill

By military necessity, and for your own safety and comfort, you and your family are enemy nationals and are hereby ordered to live in the Civil Assembly Centre. There every comfort of Western culture will be yours . . . (Instructions given to British and American nationals by the Japanese authorities, 1942)[66]

In September 1943, as the Paulson family were travelling across country and attempting to leave China, Philip was still interned at Temple Hill. Then came word that all residents were to be moved to a larger compound near Weihsien, about one hundred miles inland. Major Kosaka travelled to inspect the new camp and, upon his return, advised the internees to take everything they could, given the deplorable conditions of the new camp. Hurriedly the children and teachers packed their few belongings. Then, on September 7th, the children lined up and marched out the gate at Temple Hill, singing "God is still on the Throne," just as they had done when leaving Chefoo. Once outside the gates, they were loaded onto army trucks and driven to the harbour. The trip to Weihsien took several days. First the group travelled down the coast by boat to Tsingtao, then inland by train.

At the dock, everyone boarded a small, rusty, battered Japanese steamer. Passengers were quickly stowed in the hold, along with their luggage. The Japanese did not provide any food for the voyage. Fortunately, a Chinese baker and former mission employee had been supplying bread to the residents at Temple Hill and agreed to deliver some bread to the ship. But when the ship was ready to leave, the baker was nowhere to be seen. As hope faded, a small launch was observed approaching the departing ship. The bread had arrived!

---

[66] Austin, p. 267.

After a few sandwiches for supper, the group prepared for bed. Along the sides of the hold were two long wooden benches on which the children and staff lay, huddled side by side for sleep. The boards were hard and uncomfortable, and the hold was cold and damp. There were no toilet facilities. Rats scurried over them during the night. There was no lighting and the portholes were covered by thick sacking. An improvised curtain divided the boys from the girls.

Travelling through the Yellow Sea was dangerous at this time of year due to typhoons and storms, but, on this trip, the sea was unusually calm. However, there was still the danger of mines left by the American navy and discovery by American submarines.

On the third day the steamer arrived at Tsingtao. Upon docking, the children collected their belongings and carried them to the railway station for the next leg of their journey. On their way, they passed a number of Chinese students who showed them their contempt by spitting on the ground.

Quickly the children were herded onto the train for their trip to Weihsien, another 130 miles inland from Tsingtao. As they left the station, Major Kosaka stood at attention at the end of the railway platform and saluted. Seven hours later, without any food to eat or water to drink, they arrived in the old walled city of Weihsien, a city of about 100,000 people. Their luggage was thrown out the windows of the train and everyone had to scramble to find their belongings in the few minutes allowed before they were herded onto open-backed trucks to take them to Weihsien compound. A Japanese guard barked commands at them, which, of course, they could not understand. A lorry carried the luggage and some of the older boys and men.

Weihsien Civilian Internment Centre in Shantung Province was located three miles from the railway station and two miles northeast of Weihsien. With everyone now crammed into trucks, the group wound their way through the cobbled streets of Weihsien, out through the large city gate and into the countryside. The landscape was flat farming country with a few outcroppings of trees. After an uncomfortable forty-minute drive, the entourage proceeded down an avenue lined with Juniper trees and up to a large Chinese gate on which was written three Chinese characters that read, "Le Dao Yuan," or "Courtyard of the Happy Way." In contrast to its name, Japanese soldiers holding rifles with bared bayonets stood on guard. It was 5:00 p.m. They had arrived at their new home.

Florence: A Missionary in China

A six-foot-high brick wall surrounded the compound. Circular guard towers had been erected at each corner or bend[67] of the wall with openings for machine guns. Searchlights were mounted on the towers, and coiled, electrified barbed wire ran along the top of the wall. A large trench had been dug outside the wall. Later, more electrified barbed wire would be added outside the trench.

The compound was small, only 150 by 200 yards. Originally it had been an American Presbyterian Mission compound. Its central feature was a large brick Edwardian-style church with a red-tiled roof. In the early 1900s, the compound also had: a hospital; a seminary consisting of several large classroom buildings; a sports field; a number of large American-style brick homes for the missionaries, teachers, and doctors who worked at the compound; and a series of tiny flats, nine feet by twelve feet, for the housing of Bible students. A few trees around the buildings provided some shade from the hot summer sun. Pearl Buck, the famous American novelist, whose stories depicted the life and culture of the Chinese people, and Henry Luce, the co-founder of *Time*, *Life*, and *Fortune* magazines, were born there.

After the Presbyterian missionaries left, neglect and looting Chinese bandits destroyed the compound. Later, Japanese soldiers occupied the space. When the soldiers vacated the premises, the property was left to deteriorate further. Although all the buildings were structurally intact, their interiors had been decimated and their contents thrown outside: strewn over the grounds were old beds and radiators, bits of piping, and broken desks and classroom chairs.

When the first internees were brought to the compound, some six months before the Chefoo School, they quickly organized the site for camp life. They constructed a crude bakery and organized three huge kitchens, each with a dining hall that catered to some four to six hundred internees. The hospital, which was littered several feet deep with debris, was cleaned out and sanitized, and within ten days was up and functioning so as to feed and house patients, provide for their care, and perform simple operations, including delivering babies. Although the Japanese supplied a few basic medications, the rest had to be smuggled in as needed. All the major buildings had a few

---

[67] As a means of keeping out evil spirits, the Chinese did not employ straight lines when erecting a structure, believing that evil spirits could only go straight.

dim electrical lights, but there was no running water anywhere or sufficient means of heating the buildings. With the approach of winter, the Japanese provided little block stoves while camp engineers fashioned stovepipes from spliced jam tins fitted together. Peanut oil tins were used as makeshift ovens.

Toilet facilities in the camp were even more primitive. Servicing the 2,000 internees were only one latrine for women and three for men. In each of these latrines were five or six toilets, which were sunk into the ground and over which the internees had to squat to relieve themselves. Usually there were long queues to use the facilities, and excrement quickly mounted until it reached the top of the toilet bowls and started to flow over. Graciously, a few of the Catholic priests and nuns, and some of the Protestant missionaries tied cloths around their faces, borrowed boots and cleaning supplies, and completed a thorough clean-up. For a while they also provided daily maintenance of the facilities until a group of camp engineers devised a method of flushing the toilets after each use with a half bucket of water.

The camp began at the high wooden gate marking the entrance to the compound and proceeded down a dusty block cinder road, which the internees called "Main Street." A parallel thoroughfare was called "Tin Pan Alley." On either side of the road were rows upon rows of adjoining small cell-like rooms, nine feet by twelve feet, each with a door to the outside and a small open window[68] intended originally for the Presbyterian Bible students. The Japanese quarters were at the end of Main Street, and to the east of the row houses was the hospital.

Once functional, the internees established various committees to oversee the effective running of the camp. Nine committees, or departments, were formed, including discipline, engineering, education, finance, general affairs (comprising entertainment and athletics), labour, medicine, accommodation or quarters, and supplies.

When Philip and his fellow students arrived at Weihsien, hundreds of internees—residents of the camp—came out and enthusiastically greeted them. Approximately six months earlier the Japanese army had rounded up a varied group of foreigners: Americans, Russians, Greeks, and British from Japanese-occupied North China—Peking, Tientsin, and Tsingtao. The

---

[68] Windows in China were simple frames open to the air or covered with vegetable fibre paper, which was actually quite insulating.

group included medical doctors and professors from medical colleges and universities, missionaries and officers of the Salvation Army, entertainers and dance troupes, bankers and business executives, tourists, and priests and nuns from Manchuria. There was even a jazz band that happened to be playing in a Tientsin nightclub when they were rounded up. In all, the group now comprised about 1,800 to 2,000 people, a third of whom were children. In addition to the Chefoo students, other school children were interned at the camp. They were from an American school in Peking, and included primary and secondary school students. There was also an English grammar school from Tientsin and a group of kindergarten children.

For their first night in camp, the children ate at kitchen number one. The menu was onion soup, dried bread, pudding made with flour and water, and tea. A little bit of sugar was included as a special treat for the newcomers. The children were so hungry they thought it was a good meal. That night, and for the next three weeks, they slept in borrowed rugs and coats as they waited for their luggage to be sorted out. By the time their belongings were delivered, most of it had been rifled through and some had been looted.

To the children, the camp was an alien world. They were now seeing women in high heels and lipstick, and hearing about sex trade workers. David Michell, a Chefoo student, remembered walking into camp at the age of nine: "We had never seen people who dressed differently—or (encountered) their language. We didn't know what was swearing and what wasn't swearing. We had never heard swearing. So we had some very interesting adjustments to the outside world." (Austin, p. 279)

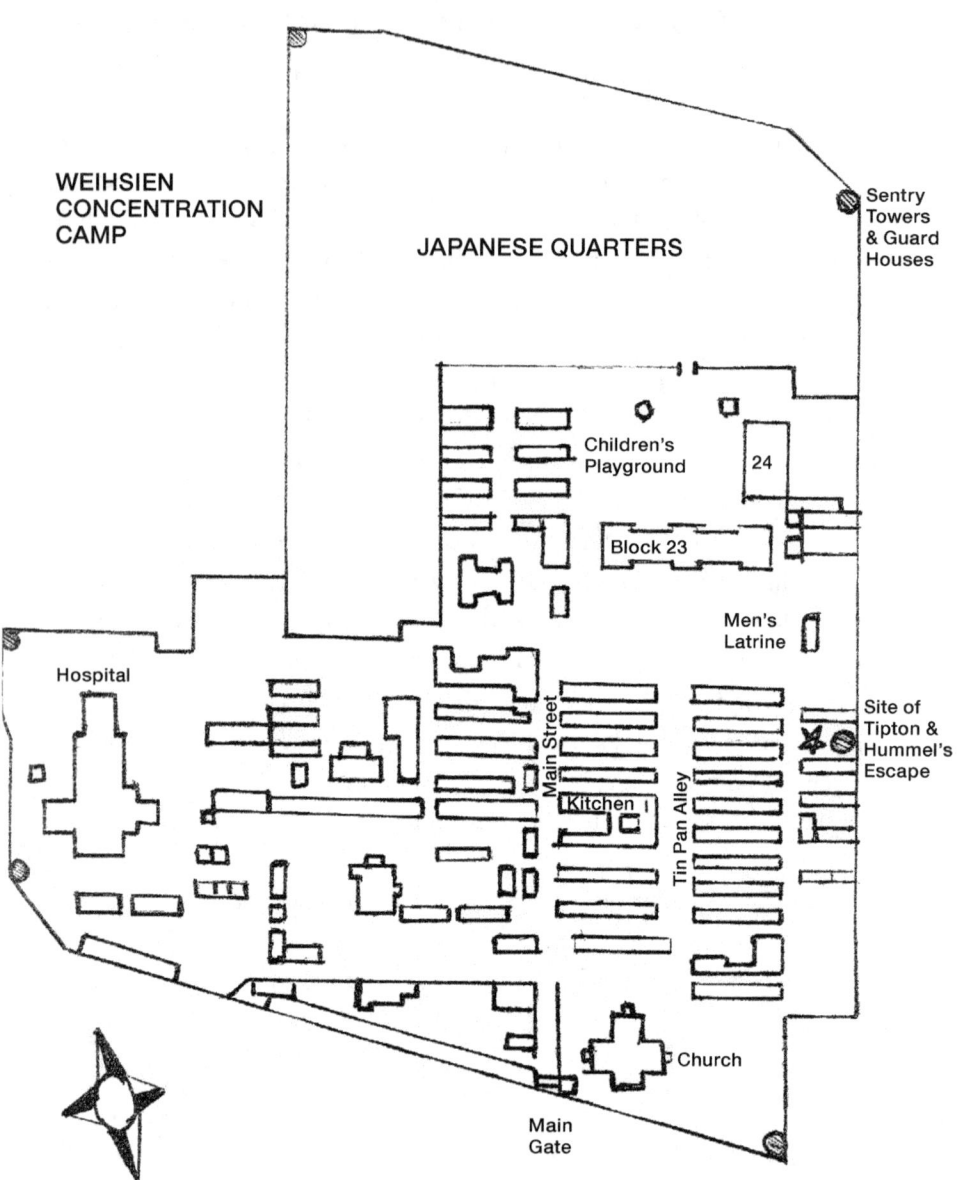

Weihsien compound in Shantung Province where Philip was interned during World War II

XXVI

Weihsien

> . . . for I have learned, in whatsoever state I am, therewith to be content.
> (Philippians 4:11)

Initially Philip and the younger children, along with their teachers, were assigned to two rooms in the basement of Block 24. Under the American Presbyterian Mission, the building had originally been one of several large school buildings. Later the children were moved into three rooms at the west end of Block 23: one room housed the male students, another the female students, and the third room their teachers.

The rooms were small, only twelve feet by sixteen. Philip and eight other little boys lined up their bedding along parallel walls. In the middle they set up their trunks, which served as seats, tables, and a play area. All in all, this one tiny room served as their bedroom, living room, playroom, and classroom. At one end of the room was a bench on which they placed their washbasins. At the other end was a small mud brick stove in which they burned little handmade coal balls and whatever twigs and wood they could scrounge to keep themselves warm in the cold weather. Often they would burn their legs in the process. A used kerosene tin provided by the Catholic sisters served as an oven.

Outside their window was one of the camp's sewage ditches. Every day coolies, with buckets hanging on each end of a pole slung across their shoulders, would arrive and fill their pails with excrement, which the Chinese called "night soil," to spread on nearby farms. The stench was nauseating.

The other Chefoo arrivals were housed at various places around the compound. Single men and women were assigned to dormitory rooms in the remaining school buildings, while married couples and their children were housed in the little nine- by twelve-foot rooms. In the dormitories, a person's personal space amounted to six feet by three feet, just enough space for a bedroll and the odd personal item.

The routine in the camp was established according to camp rules, chores, mealtimes, and daily activities. The children got up early to fetch and heat water for washing. Then, at 7:00 a.m., the camp bell rang for daily roll call. At various parts of the camp the internees assembled to be counted. The time it took for count varied, with the longest being five and a half hours. Later in the day there would be a second roll call.

After count, everyone queued up for breakfast at their respective dining hall with bowl and spoon in hand. Each person had to supply his or her own cup, bowl or plate, as well as cutlery. Often tin cans or even soap dishes served as mugs or bowls. The line for meals was usually long, sometimes stretching as far as seventy yards with a wait time of three quarters of an hour.

Breakfast was usually a small bowl of coarse bread, millet or sorghum porridge and two slices of hard bread. Mugs were filled with black tea ladled out of a bucket. The tea was always weak as the cooks re-used the leaves over and over in an attempt to extract every last bit of flavour from them. After breakfast, everyone lined up again to have their bowls and spoons washed.

The children then returned to their rooms to clean and to hang their bedding out in the sun in an attempt to kill bed bugs, lice, and fleas. Laundry was done three days each week. Everyone had to work. One of the children's jobs was to carry the wet laundry from the hospital, where it had been scrubbed by hand, often without soap, back to their rooms in Block 23. The children carried the basins of wet washing on their heads or in their arms and delivered them to the teachers to be hung out on the line.

Philip had other chores, one of which was sifting through the ash heaps for pieces of unburned coal, and to gather sticks or anything else that could be burned in their stove to keep them warm at night and during the winter. The Japanese also provided coal dust for the stoves, but it could not be burned in dust form; it had to be sifted and mixed with clay and water, pressed together, and then put in the sun to dry as coal bricks. Philip and the other children were also responsible for transporting water from the pump house to various parts of the camp, and peeling vegetables in the kitchen. The students, used to firm discipline, responded well to their assigned chores, and they and their staff were considered the "best organized and most efficient group of all in camp"[69]

After chores, the children had their school lessons. They sat on their trunks while their teachers taught them the required subjects, all by memory. With paper being scarce, the children wrote their assignments in pencil and erased them after they were marked. They did this until the pages were completely erased through. The teachers made every effort to keep the students on track for the Oxford University matriculation exams. While at Weihsien, three classes took the exams. The teachers devised the tests from previous ones, and all the test forms and answers were carefully kept and submitted to England for assessment after the war. The children's exams were all accepted in England, and showed positive results.

During the day, the children lined up again for dinner, which usually consisted of hash or stew and bread. Supper consisted of thin soup, which was often a watered down version of the stew from dinner, and more bread. The meals were referred to as "S.O.S.," meaning "same old slop." Because this diet was sorely lacking in calcium, the shells from black market eggs were collected and ground into powder and fed to the children by the spoonful.

Philip and his little group of friends ate in kitchen number one, which contained a large dining room with long, rough-hewn wooden tables and benches. Frequently the hall filled with the stench of the open sewage cesspools, which wafted everywhere. Despite being in camp, the teachers still insisted on exhibiting table manners at each meal. Though their fare was meagre, the rules were clear:

> Sit up straight. Don't stuff food into your mouth. Don't talk with your mouth full. Don't drink when you have food in your mouth. Keep your voices down. Don't complain . . . (The example of St. Paul was referenced time and time again). "For I have learned in whatsoever state I am, therewith to be content." We were God's representatives in this concentration camp, our teachers said, and God was not represented well by rudeness.[70]

---

[69] Miller, p. 152.
[70] Michell, p. 82.

After supper there was a bit of free time for play and other activities. Outside games were somewhat curtailed, however, by soldiers with German Shepherds who patrolled the grounds at night.

The food at Weihsien was inadequate, lacking in nutrition and quantity. What there was had to be prepared from the basest forms: grain had to be ground into flour for bread, which was the main staple of the camp. There were slices of bread, bread porridge, and bread pudding. Initially bread was not rationed, but by 1944 only two slices of bread were allowed per meal, with breakfast sometimes consisting of two slices of bread and a cup of hot water. Lunch was two slices of bread and a bowl of stew, while supper was two slices of bread and a cup of thin soup.

Water had to be pumped and boiled for cooking and drinking. Internees worked half hour shifts that involved manipulating a three-foot metal handle to coax water from a well into one of four forty-gallon drums. The pumps were manned from six in the morning until nine at night. Then the water had to be carried to the kitchen.

Fuel had to be prepared from the coal dust and fires built to cook the food. Big fifty-gallon cauldrons were placed over the fire for the cooking of soups and stews. Sometimes a large, shallow wok was used. Occasionally, when stirring the contents, the cooks had to stand so close to the open fire that their clothing started to burn and the fumes and smoke singed their nostrils.

Vegetables, if any, had to be peeled and washed. The vegetables usually consisted of gnarled potatoes, bitter-tasting Chinese greens, and some rotting eggplant. Weeds were collected from the compound and also cooked as a vegetable. Meat, like vegetables, was usually half spoiled and maggot-ridden, and consisted of horse or mule and included skin, fat, and innards. It had to be boiled immediately before it went completely rotten. Even in its rotten state, what meat they had was very limited, with one dead pig having to last for a week for the whole camp. Even fish bones were fried for food. Each morning provisions for the day were driven into the compound, to a central supply house, and then distributed to each kitchen. Besides the meagre supplies of rotting meat, the Japanese also provided millet, soya, lu-dou (a coarse sort of bean), and sorghum. The sorghum was a reddish brown cereal crop used mainly for chicken feed. It had to be ground and then boiled until it produced a tasteless type of brown porridge.

Florence: A Missionary in China

Sometimes food ran out and people who had queued up were turned away. Seconds were rare. When one little girl discovered that she was allowed a second drink of water at playtime, she shouted excitedly, "Hey everybody, seconds on water."[71]

Everyone lived with the pangs of hunger and the spectre of future starvation. There was malnutrition and diseases were prevalent—dysentery, malaria, hepatitis, typhoid, and cholera. All drinking water had to be boiled.

Given the meagre diet of everyone in camp, a black market quickly developed where cash and valuables were exchanged for eggs and other food. One method of collecting orders was for a Chinese accomplice, their body blackened and greased and clad only in a loin cloth, to climb over the wall at night and pick up the shopping list and monies. Methods of delivery varied. Cabbages and live chickens were thrown over the electric fence, while eggs were passed through holes in the wall or placed on top of the wall, just under the electrified fence. One of the chief egg suppliers was a Chinese Christian lady called Mrs. Kang. At night, with the help of her young sons, she would funnel a steady stream of eggs into a drainage tunnel that came in underneath the wall. One of the camp residents would then crawl into the drain to obtain the smuggled goods. The Catholic priests were pivotal players in the black market—not for personal gain but as a humanitarian effort. They would stand at the wall, looking as though they were praying, and then hide the eggs under their robes. Lookouts were stationed to keep watch for the Japanese guards. If one approached, the lookout blew his nose loudly to alert the others.

Father Scanlan, an Australian Trappist monk, was the most memorable black marketeer. He and four other Trappist monks shared a room very close to the outside wall, which was an excellent location for the smuggling activities. All of his dealings were recorded in what he called "The Book of Life." One time he was involved in bringing a basket of eggs over the wall when a guard chanced by. Keeping his presence of mind, Scanlan quietly took down some laundry that was hanging on a line to dry and carefully laid it over the basket. He continued pulling down articles of clothing until the unsuspecting guard passed by. (Cliff, p. 79)

Another time, Scanlan arranged for a delivery of eggs through the drainage tunnel. A Japanese guard came upon him as he was busy collecting the eggs

---

[71] Michell, p. 71.

in a wooden box. Quickly, Scanlan put the box against the opening of the tunnel and, spreading his gown over the box, sat down. He crossed himself and started chanting in Latin, trying to appear as unassuming as possible. But the eggs kept coming through the drainage tunnel, one by one, and started to break against the wooden box. Scanlan chanted louder in an effort to hide the noise of the cracking eggs and, in Latin, called for the other priests to come help him, which they promptly did.

"One evening he was caught black marketeering, was arrested and taken towards the guardroom for questioning. Realising that he had a lot of money in his pocket from his nefarious activities, he staged a fall into the public toilet. Out of sight for a moment from his captors, he shed the white gown he had been wearing and with it his funds, and emerged from the W.C. in the black gown he had been wearing under his white one. What was more, he was now surrounded by other internees, also emerging from the toilet. The guards lost sight of him in the crowd with his sudden change of uniform." (Cliff, p. 80)

Finally, Father Scanlan was caught and was unable to escape punishment. He was given time in solitary confinement, which provided major amusement for the other internees. Prior to his internment at Weihsien, Scanlan, as a Trappist monk, had been living in a cave outside Peking for fifteen years under a vow of silence. At Weihsien, he had received special dispensation from his bishop for suspension of his silence. For him, solitary confinement was not a punishment. In solitary he decided to sing his Latin prayers aloud late at night. And as his cell was in one of the buildings housing soldiers, his singing kept them awake. De Jaegher, a fellow priest, recounted the unfolding of events.

> Shortly before midnight the Japanese officers were awakened by the rich stentorian tones of a baritone voice chanting:
> "Deus, in adjutorium meum intende.
> Domine, ad adjuvandum me festina."
>
> It was Father Scanlan singing his office at the top of his voice, yelling in Latin:
> "Lord, come to my aid.
> Lord, come quickly to my aid. . ."
>
> Father Scanlan went on from the matins, continuing in his loudest tones:
> "Domine, quam multi sunt qui tribulant!
> Me multi insurgunt adversum me! . . ."

Florence: A Missionary in China

"How many there are who trouble me!
How many are there who are against me!"

On and on Father Scanlan went, putting all his heart and soul and voice into his office:
"In te, Domine, speravi:
Non confundar in aetornum."

Giving voice to his own faith as he sang:
"In you Lord, I have hoped:
I will not be deceived forever."

"An hour had gone by now, and the Japanese were getting restless. At first they had been sure this was only a momentary aberration on the part of this great red-faced, red-haired foreigner, but now, after an hour, when he showed no signs of letdown, either in volume or enthusiasm,"[72] they went to investigate. Upon learning that these noisy activities were his obligatory religious exercises, and being superstitious about interfering with someone's religious practices, they hesitated to intrude. Of course, Father Scanlon did not inform them that he could have chosen another time to recite his prayers, or that he could have even recited them silently to himself. After eight nights of interrupted sleep, the Japanese officers decided to release him from solitary confinement and sent him back to camp.

For internees, the usual punishment for black marketeering was one or two weeks in solitary confinement. For the Chinese it was death. One Chinese was electrocuted while trying to smuggle in food. His body was left to hang on the electric fence in the sports field as a gruesome warning to others.

In January 1945, the American Red Cross provided care packages to the camp. Each internee received a heavy cardboard box measuring three feet by one foot by one and a half feet. These boxes contained powdered milk, cigarettes,[73] tinned butter, spam, cheese, chocolate, sugar, coffee, canned salmon, and raisins. Philip was ecstatic and quickly traded his cigarettes and

---

[72] De Jaegher, pp. 250–251.
[73] One source of contention between the secular camp residents and the missionaries was that, given their disapproval of smoking, the missionaries refused to loan out their ration cards for allotted cigarettes. That said, they were more than willing to trade the cigarettes in their Red Cross care packages for food.

151

coffee for additional food items; at that time, one package of cigarettes could be bartered for two bars of chocolate.

The only other source of additional food or supplies was a small camp canteen stocked by the Japanese where certain bare necessities could be bought in exchange for money or valuables. The canteen stocked such items as peanuts, peanut oil for cooking and burning in lamps, soap, and toilet paper.

In his book, *Saving China*, Alvyn Austin recounted the internees' preoccupation with getting enough to eat:

> As their clothing became frayed and the mosquito netting ripped, as the tin cups lost their enamel and the shoes their soles, the people had nothing with which to replace them. In such poverty, where a used sardine can was worth its weight in gold—as a cup, a shovel, a toy for the children, or a safety-deposit container—food became the main preoccupation. (Austin, p. 281)

Although adequate food was of primary concern, clothing was also of great importance. The clothes in which the children had arrived had long since become rags or had been outgrown. In summer the children wore shorts and went barefoot, as shoes were saved for winter. A repair and mending shop had been set up in the camp for repairing shoes and making clothes. Shoes were patched until finally there was nothing left to repair. New shirts and dresses were made from old curtains and mattress covers; trousers were made from cut-up blankets and underwear from tablecloths. Still the clothing was not really warm and everyone was always cold. Philip actually sold his only pair of shoes for an egg. Then there were the plagues of vermin to contend with: flies and mosquitoes buzzed around incessantly, bedbugs in the mattresses constantly bit them, and rats ran over them at night.

Obtaining medicinal supplies for the hospital was another major problem, though ingenuity generally prevailed. One such instance involved Laurence Tipton, a business executive, and Eric Hummel, an English teacher, both of whom had escaped from the camp. The two arranged for a large quantity of much-needed antibiotic sulfa drugs for the hospital. The major problem was getting them into the camp as they were contained in four large crates of obvious Allied origin, and the only official person allowed into the camp was the Swiss consul from Tsingtao, Mr. Laubscher. Initially, Mr. Laubscher thought the task was impossible, but he quickly devised a very clever scheme. First he had his secretary type out a list of all the drugs that could be legitimately obtained in Tsingtao, but leave four spaces between each item on the list. Then Laubscher took the list to the Japanese police for approval, which was readily obtained. Next he had his secretary fill in the blank spaces with the names of all the drugs in the crates. With the official seal on the list, the crates of drugs entered the camp and were successfully delivered to the hospital.

The only bright spots in camp life were the occasional evening and weekend activities organized by the internees. There were pantomimes, plays, choral programmes, and symphony concerts with such performances as Handel's *Messiah*, Stainer's *The Crucifixion*, Maunder's *Olivet to Calvary*, and Mozart's *Concerto in D Minor* (minus double basses and tubas), as well as full-scale performances of Shaw's *Androcles and The Lion*. The play was staged, according to one camp internee, with "three complete sets, a full size lion made of cloth and cardboard, and armor and helmets for ten Roman guards soldered together out of tin cans from the Red Cross parcels."[74] There were even performances by the black jazz band.

The camp had its own choir, which was organized by Mrs. Bazire of the CIM, and a Salvation Army band that practiced every Tuesday evening. One of the band members composed a medley of all the Allied national anthems, which was practiced in small segments so as not to be recognized by the Japanese. The objective was to play it when the camp was liberated. However, when the time actually came for it to be played, the band members initially forgot to do so.

Evening educational classes were also organized. Some of the brightest minds in North China were interned at Weihsien: professors, medical doctors, missionaries, and business people from a variety of backgrounds. Utilizing their expertise, over a hundred adult education classes were provided to the camp in a variety of languages—Chinese, Japanese, English, Russian, and French—and on a number of subjects, including religion, mathematics, art, history, and philosophy.

On Saturday nights there was usually a play or a concert. Sundays included a variety of church services. In the morning there was a Roman Catholic

---

[74] Gilkey, p. 70.

Mass, as Catholics comprised the largest denomination in camp, and then an Anglican service. In the afternoon an interdenominational service was provided by the Protestant denominations. After the service, the Salvation Army band played hymns in the open square, followed by audience requests. Then the band played another hour outside the hospital, for the patients' benefit. Friday night was a prayer meeting for all those interested, and a youth group for the adolescent internees. Eric Lidell, a British missionary and famous Olympian sprinter, ran the youth group. In the sports field there were races, baseball, volleyball, and soccer games—sometimes with Catholic priests pitted against Protestant missionaries—and Boy Scout and Girl Guide meetings. The children even organized their own entertainment. There were rat and fly catching competitions, and the sizzling of bedbugs over candles made from wax given to them by the Catholic sisters. The candles were also used to fry old bread crusts scrounged from one of the kitchens for an evening snack.

XXVII

Eric Liddell

. . . for them that honour me I will honour . . . (I Samuel 2:30)

Probably one of the most famous internees at Weihsien was Eric Liddell. Eric was born in January 1902 in China, to missionary parents James and Mary Liddell, of the London Missionary Society. After spending his early years in China, Eric returned to his parents' homeland of Scotland and was educated at Eltham College and the University of Edinburgh. He played rugby and was a world-class runner in the one hundred-metre sprint, in which he was entered at the 1924 Olympics in Paris. However, when they announced the schedule for the one hundred-metre heats, and Eric learned they were to be run on a Sunday, he refused to participate—it was against his religious principles to engage in sports on the Lord's Day. The British athletics authorities were horrified and the press condemned him as a traitor to his country. At that point, he was asked to train for the four hundred metres, one of the toughest of races, requiring the runner to go at a sprint the entire way.

Prior to the race, Liddell's masseur gave him a note that read, "In the old book it says, 'He that honours me I will honour.' Wishing you the best of success always!"[75] In the race Eric drew the outside lane—the worst possible lane for a novice as the runner had to set his own pace without the benefit of knowing how his opponents were faring. Despite his running lane and the distance of the race, which is totally unsuited for a one hundred-metre sprinter, Eric not only won a gold medal in the four hundred metres but also set a world record. His story is immortalized in the movie *Chariots of Fire*, which won an Academy Award for Best Picture in 1981.

---

[75] Magnusson, p. 52.

Eric's goal, however, was not to pursue an athletic career but to return to China as a missionary. And in the summer of 1925, he did so, returning to the land of his birth under the same mission as his parents. As an educational missionary he joined the staff of the Anglo-Chinese College in Tientsin, a Christian middle school for about five hundred boys, where he taught science and athletics for over ten years.

While teaching in Tientsin, he was invited by Japan to compete in an athletic competition with Olympic athletes from France and Japan. This international sports event in Manchuria was organized by Japan in 1928, in connection with the coronation of the new emperor of Japan. Eric was twenty-seven years old and physically fit, and easily won the two hundred- and four hundred-metre races. His final race was scheduled at 2:45 p.m. but his ship was to leave at 3:00 p.m. to return to Tientsin, so Eric arranged for a taxi to pick him up at the finish line. Eric crossed the finish line and continued running to the waiting taxi, but just as he was about to step into it, the British National Anthem started to play, forcing him to stand at attention. Next came the Marseillaise, which forced him to continue standing even longer. But the moment the second anthem finished, Eric jumped into the taxi and they sped to the wharf. By the time he reached the dock the boat was already fifty feet out, but he could see that it would have to round the corner of the dock, coming closer to him as it proceeded out of the harbour. Jumping over crates and other obstructions, he raced to the edge of the dock. Just then, a huge wave brought the boat to within fifteen feet. Eric quickly hurled his bags on board and then, with one gigantic leap, jumped toward the moving boat, successful grabbing onto a railing and pulling himself aboard.

In 1934, Eric married Florence McKenzie, the daughter of Canadian missionaries also working in Tientsin. Two daughters were born soon after. Later, because of the need for evangelistic work in the country, Eric went to southern Hopei as an itinerant missionary. With harsh conditions and continuing wars ravaging the country, Eric made arrangements for his wife, now pregnant with their third child, to leave China for the safety of Canada. He planned to follow her several months later. Back in Canada, Florence gave birth to their third daughter. However, before Eric could leave China he was placed under house arrest and, in late March 1943, was sent with other enemy nationals to Weihsien. Philip and the rest of the Chefoo school followed some six months later. Eric was housed on the second storey of Block 23, above

Florence: A Missionary in China

Philip and the other young boys, and was the warden for Blocks 23 and 24. It was his job to collect supplies for the 230 people in his area, and to make sure everyone was in place for the morning and evening roll calls.

Eric had other responsibilities as well. As chairman of the Recreation Committee he helped organize all athletic events: arranging the activities, organizing the teams, and looking after the equipment. He also worked with the teachers there in arranging sports days for the students. He umpired their soccer games, taught the children to play basketball and rounders, and organized chess and draughts tournaments and dart contests. On Thursday afternoons he looked after the younger students, including Philip, in order to give the teachers a break, and on Friday evenings he ran a youth club. Then, on Sundays, he taught Bible class. Eric was also part of the Education Committee and was assigned to the school as a math and science teacher. From memory, he created a one hundred-page chemistry book and talked the students through each experiment. Philip remembered him as a good teacher.

Eric was known for his kindness, quiet manner, and humility—a real servant of God. Norman Cliff, a student at Weihsien, said, "If there were a call to preach, to coach, to help, to advise, he was there, however busy or tired he might be."[76] A White Russian prostitute said, after Eric installed a shelf in her room, that he was the only man who ever did anything for her without asking for favours in return. Regardless of fatigue, he carried buckets of water to the rooms of the sick and the elderly, and in winter, he brought in coal dust from which fuel pellets were made.

In December 1944, Eric started experiencing severe headaches and was slowing down considerably. In hospital, in his last hour before succumbing to a brain tumour, he wrote out the words of his favourite hymn:

> Be still, my soul, the Lord is on thy side;
> Bear patiently the cross of grief or pain;
> Leave to thy God to order and provide;
> In every change He will remain.
> Be still, my soul, thy best, thy heavenly Friend
> Through thorny ways leads to a joyful end.[77]

---

[76] Cliff, p. 82.
[77] Written by Kathrina Von Schlegel.

Eric died on February 21, 1945, as the evening snow gently fell on Weihsien. His last words were, "It is complete surrender." He was forty-three.

His funeral was held on Saturday, February 24th, in the Edwardian-style church on the compound. It was a bleak, windswept day. People from all over the camp crowded into the church for the service, and those who couldn't get in stood outside. Those inside waited in silence while the song "I Know That My Redeemer Liveth" resounded throughout the chapel. The children from Chefoo school made a wreath for the service. A tribute, a prayer, a hymn, the Lord's Prayer, the Benediction, and a closing—"O Rest in the Lord"—and the funeral service was over. Then Eric's friends bore the coffin through an honour guard of students, taking him to the quiet cemetery that lay within the Japanese quarters. All of the students, including Philip, stood at attention. His body was lowered into the ground as the beatitudes were repeated: "Blessed are the meek, for they shall inherit the earth. Blessed are the pure in heart; for they shall see God . . ."

His grave was marked with a simple cross with his name written on it in shoe polish.

XXVIII

Tipton and Hummel

And I will deliver thee out of the hand of the wicked, and I will redeem thee out of the hand of the terrible. (Jeremiah 5:21)

In June 1944, two men escaped from Weihsien. One was Laurance Tipton, an Englishman employed by the British-American Tobacco Company, and the other was Arthur Hummel,[78] an American who had been teaching English at the Fu Jen Catholic University in Peking.

After working for ten years in China, Tipton was fluent in Chinese and well travelled in the northeast part of the country. During the Japanese occupation of Peking, Tipton was confined to the city and, like all other enemy nationals, required to wear a red armband bearing Chinese characters denoting his respective nationality. In March 1942, the foreign nationals were informed that they were being sent to Weihsien.

The Japanese Embassy issued a prospectus that read more like an advertisement for a summer camp than an internment centre. As Tipton reported,

> We learned that there would be ample food provided, fresh vegetables and fruit in season, including strawberries; there was a dairy and milk would be supplied to the children, nursing mothers and the aged. Accommodation was spacious, but we were advised to take bed and bedding and eating utensils. Small supplies of additional food could also be taken. Recreational facilities were provided and one should take tennis rackets, balls, etc. There would be conducted walks in the country and to the town for shopping, but a canteen would also be established within the Assembly Centre, at which purchases of daily

---
[78] Arthur Hummel later became the American Ambassador to China from 1981–1985.

necessities could be made. Cameras and radio sets were prohibited. One gramophone could be taken for every twenty guests. (Tipton, p. 66)

Despite the luxurious account of Weihsien, a committee formed among Peking residents provided more useful suggestions on what should be taken, including: mosquito nets, tin plates and mugs, carpentry tools and nails, cooking utensils, books, writing paper and typewriters, medicinal supplies, warm clothing and footwear, soap, and canned food. Each person was allowed to take two trunks and a bedding crate. On March 29th, Tipton and the other British citizens left Peking by train, bound for Weihsien.

At Weihsien, Tipton's associates were other internees interested in the happenings of the war. This small group was comprised of: Father de Jaegher, a Jesuit Belgian priest; Roy Tchou, a tall Eurasian man from Tientsin; and Tommy Wade, also an employee of the British-American Tobacco Company. Eventually their talk turned to escape from Weihsien. Through the illicit mail system, information was collected from friends in the area about the countryside, and the locations of enemy and friendly forces. Maps were also obtained.

De Jaegher was in charge of the underground mail delivery system in camp. In an attempt to get mail out of the camp he had a craftsman from the camp fashion a metal box with a water-tight sliding lid. Outgoing letters would be placed in the box, which would then be placed discreetly in one of the cesspool buckets carried out by the coolies. Once outside the compound, the box would be opened and the mail forwarded to its destinations.

Other forms of communication also existed, again using the coolies who collected waste from the camp. Messages from the outside were written in code on fine silk formed into a pellet and encapsulated in a contraceptive rubber, which the coolie would put up his nose or hold in his mouth. At some point during his work, the coolie would blow his nose or spit. Watched carefully by several internees, the pellet would be retrieved and delivered to a designated translator in the camp—usually a discreet missionary. Outgoing messages were delivered in the same manner, although written on silk from the cast-off underwear of some of the camp women.

Close calls were frequent. One time, a guard doing a routine check forced a coolie to open his mouth, whereupon the coolie promptly swallowed the pellet. An internee watching the incident quickly ran to the hospital and procured a sizeable amount of castor oil, which was secretly administered to the coolie. Later, after the castor oil had worked its magic, the pellet was successfully retrieved. If the coolie had been caught with the pellet, he would have been summarily executed.

Through correspondence with the outside, Tipton learned that only Weihsien and a surrounding area of fifteen to twenty miles were actually controlled by the Japanese. A large Japanese garrison stationed at Fangtze, a railway town about five miles southeast of the camp, was responsible for the area; however, stationed outside the perimeter were isolated groups of Communists and Nationalist guerrilla units. Some of these local guerrillas were ex-Chinese army veterans who had not fled with the retreating Nationalist Army but had decided to stay and protect their farmlands and villages from Japanese pillaging. Others were simply Chinese patriots. Eventually Tipton was able to make contact with a commander of a Chinese guerrilla unit based in a northern part of Shantung Province. A plan was devised for Tipton and de Jaegher to escape and meet with him.

The actual plan for the breakout took one year to formulate. The final plan set June 9th or 10th as the date of flight. On either day, the moon would rise late, giving the men one hour of darkness to get over the wall, but be bright enough later on to illuminate their way through the countryside. They chose 9:00 p.m. for the escape, which coincided with the darkness and was before the moon's ascent and the changing of guards at the watchtowers. Typically the guard coming on duty would make a routine inspection of the area and then take a ten-minute break for a cup of tea and a cigarette before mounting his watchtower. It was during this short period of time that Tipton and de Jaegher concluded they would have to enact their plan.

They selected as the location for their escape the watchtower in the middle of the west wall, as that particular section of wall had a bend in it that obscured it from the searchlights. A rendezvous was set for a thickly wooded cemetery several miles northeast of the camp between nine and midnight. There, a small band of guerrillas disguised as peasants would meet them and help them the rest of the way.

In an attempt to help exonerate their roommates, Tipton and de Jaegher started sleeping outside, which many did in the summer months anyway. This way, it wouldn't be necessary for the other internees to report them missing at lights out, which was at ten o'clock every night. Tipton also resigned from his cooking job in kitchen number one and asked the Labour Committee for a few days rest. Although the camp leaders were aware of the planned escape, they were not going to report the men missing until the following afternoon, in order to ensure their getaway. The two men packed knapsacks full of items they would need on the outside, as well as a typewriter, a watch, and a fountain pen, which had been requested by their rescuers. On June 8th the would-be escapees made a dry run during the daytime and were able to determine how to scale the wall without touching the electrified wire that ran along the top.

Everything was set to go, but at the last minute, a fellow priest of de Jaegher's begged him not to go for fear of reprisals impacting the rest of the camp, potentially made all the worse because he was a priest. The organizing group of Tipton, de Jaegher, Tchou, and Wade asked Arthur Hummel to take his place.

At 8:00 p.m. on June 9, 1944, Tipton and Hummel slipped into tight-fitting clothes and black Chinese jackets. Then they waited for the changing of the guards. The incoming guards arrived promptly at 9:00 p.m., but the guard at the section of the wall where the escape was to take place did not follow his usual procedure of walking his section of the wall. Instead, he remained at his post. Tipton and Hummel waited anxiously. Finally, the guard moved away from the watchtower. But just as Tipton and Hummel were about to run to the tower, they noticed two internees sitting outside facing the very area from which they intended to leave. By the time the internees went back inside their dormitory, Tipton's lookouts had lost track of the guard. They quickly decided to take their chances and try to leave anyway, making a mad dash for the tower. From there, de Jaegher, Tchou, and Wade helped Tipton and Hummel up the wall and over the live barbed wire fences. Once clear, the others threw their knapsacks over the wall. The two men dashed again, to a graveyard some fifty yards away where they flung themselves behind the first grave mound they came to. After collecting their breath, they made another short run that took them out of range of the searchlights. Gathering their bearings, they headed north to the rendezvous spot. The moon was just starting to rise in the sky, and in doing so shed some light on their surroundings.

At an old cemetery several miles from camp they met, as prearranged, a group of men also dressed in black, each carrying a German Mauser. Together they pushed on to the guerrillas' headquarters, travelling throughout the night. By dawn they had covered about twenty miles and were far away from the camp.

On Saturday the men were reported missing by Ted McClaren, one of the camp leaders. On hearing of the escape, the commandant was furious and hurriedly dispatched soldiers who scoured the countryside with police dogs, but by then the men were long gone. Roll call that day took three hours, and harsh reprisals were enforced. If any member of a group was late for count, the entire group had to remain behind an extra three quarters of an hour. Food rations were cut. The men who shared the dormitory with Tipton and Hummel were arrested, confined for ten days, and subjected to prolonged interrogations. The guards became more demanding and suspicious of everything. And because the escapees had been housed in the attic of the hospital, which was the top floor of the tallest building in camp, the area was suspected as a location for signalling to people outside the camp. Consequently, the men who still occupied it were moved out and replaced by Philip and the other boys from his dorm.

Outside the camp, with Tipton and Hummel having joined up with a band of Nationalist guerrillas, they were finally able to receive news of the war by radio and relay it back to camp. They were also able to arrange items to be smuggled into camp.

XXIX

Liberation of Weihsien

Refrain thy voice from weeping and thine eyes from tears. Your work will be rewarded. Your children will come home from the land of the enemy and they will come to their own border. (Jeremiah 31:16–17)

Camp life continued for Philip and the other internees at Weihsien. Day in and day out it was the same: chores, rules, school, lack of food, and lack of warmth.

Then, in the summer of 1945, Tipton and Hummel sent word to the camp that there were signs of a Japanese surrender. Excitement over the news was quickly tempered by the guards' threats: that if Japan surrendered, they would first kill the internees and then kill themselves. Mixed with anticipation of the war's end, there was now the fear of execution. This fear became more real when it was later learned that the Japanese had executed Catholic priests and prisoners of war when the Philippines was liberated by the Allies.

There was also the fear that the Japanese would stop all food supplies coming in to the camp and the residents would simply starve. Philip's staff decided to save any little bits of extra food that they could get in the event of such an occurrence, but not at the expense of the children. Any food that came was given to the children that same day. "The thought was that growing children need even more food than they were getting . . . (so the) staff went ahead doing all (they) could for the children, confident that (their) Shepherd was not unmindful of His own."[79]

Friday August 17th was just another routine day. At 9:00 a.m., Philip and his class assembled in the church for their weekly singing lesson. Just after the start of the lesson, they heard the sound of a plane flying low overhead.

---

[79] Thompson, p. 34.

Then someone started yelling, "American plane! American plane!" Philip and his classmates rushed to the sports field. Everywhere in camp the workday stopped as people started running outside. Upon seeing the American plane they started cheering, jumping up and down, waving their hands in the air. A few men even took off their shirts to wave.

The plane banked and circled the camp three times, flying low over the watchtowers and camp walls. Its name was clearly visible on the side of the plane: "The Armored Angel." Then about a half mile from camp, seven soldiers descended by parachute from the plane's underbelly. Seeing this, the internees ran for the front gate, which yielded easily to the mass of humanity pressing against it. Rushing past the astonished guards, the crowd pushed through the eight-foot-high corn and sorghum fields that surrounded the camp. Philip, in bare feet and shorts, ran with them. The children were faster than the adults and reached the soldiers first. Uncertain of their reception by the Japanese, the soldiers had secured themselves behind grave mounds, their guns drawn and loaded.

Still buoyant with excitement, the adults deftly picked up the soldiers and hefted them onto their shoulders, carrying them back toward the front gate of the camp. Philip and some of the other children followed behind, dragging their parachutes while shouting and cheering.

Members of the Salvation Army brass band suddenly remembered that they were to play a victory march upon their liberation. The band members quickly assembled on a mound behind the church, which commanded a clear view of the incoming procession. The band had practiced a medley of the various Allied national anthems for months; however, it had been practiced in stages so as to disguise the music from the Japanese. Now the victory march was played in full, and the crowd easily recognized its many pieces and joined in, singing alongside.

The commander of the American soldiers was a Major Staiger. Inside the front gate of the compound, Major Staiger, with a loaded service pistol in each hand, entered the Japanese guardhouse. The camp commandant handed the major his sword as a sign of surrender, and the guards quickly stacked their guns in one corner of the room. With quiet graciousness, the major handed the sword back to the commandant and, through an interpreter, informed him that they had only come to assess the situation and make arrangements to evacuate the critically ill and elderly. The major wanted the Japanese to continue providing care and security for the camp, but under American orders. The major revealed that there was fighting going on around Weihsien, between Communist and Nationalist forces, and a group of Chinese bandits were planning to capture the camp and use the internees as political hostages. A second, larger contingent of American soldiers were set to arrive later and take over camp responsibilities.

The American soldiers, in addition to the enthusiastic welcome given to them, were treated with all the deference of hero worship. Wherever the soldiers walked in camp they had a long procession of adoring admirers that followed them. Internees wanted to talk to them, touch them, or just be close to them.

For supper, two of the soldiers went to kitchen number one, where Philip ate. The cooks prepared a special meal for them drawn from reserves that had previously been used only sparingly. But quietly and politely, they left their food uneaten—food that was a treat for the internees was not adequate fare for the men.

A few days after the arrival of the American soldiers, B-29s dropped forty-four gallon drums of canned fruit near the camp. Even with two parachutes, the drums were exceedingly heavy, and many broke open when they hit the ground. When the all-clear signal was given, Philip and the other children ran into the fields and consumed tin after tin of Del Monte peaches.

The planes kept coming, though, bringing more food, clothing, and medicine. The sky was frequently full of yellow, green, red, blue, and white parachutes. Norman Cliff, one of the older Chefoo students, recalled, "The years of bread porridge, bread pudding and bread-what-have-you were now over. . . . I recalled the words of the psalmist: 'Thou spreadest a table before me in the presence of mine enemies. My cup runneth over.'" (Cliff, p. 120)

As soon as they heard a plane overhead, one of the internees would go up to the tower of Block 23 and summon others on duty for parcel collection. Once outside the camp gate, the collection crew would stand a short distance away from the drop area to avoid being hit by a falling parcel. Some of the Chinese peasants that swarmed the area, never having seen so much food in their lives, were not so fortunate. After each food drop, a group of internees would carefully record the number of parcels, as each would have to be accounted for later. The parcels were then collected and taken to the church for distribution. All of the supplies were surplus products that had initially been designated for American troops in the Pacific. With the sudden cessation of fighting there, their resources had been redirected to the internment camps in Weihsien and Shanghai. Philip's allotment at one point amounted to two towels, three handkerchiefs, one cap, four tins of food (one being chopped pork and egg yolks), two big and four small chocolate bars, ten packets of chewing gum (Chiclets and Beechnut), and ten boxes of cigarettes. Many of the food products were unknown to the children: they drank ketchup like a liquid and ate chewing gum like it was candy.

On August 20th, more American soldiers arrived, under the command of Colonel Hyman Weinburg. They had flown to a makeshift airfield about five miles from Weihsien and then driven the rest of the way by truck. Upon their arrival, they took over control of the camp from the Japanese, who again laid down their rifles, bowed their heads, and then left to join their garrison in retreat.

Next to arrive were various Chinese mayors and dignitaries from nearby villages, bringing with them cartloads of vegetables, grains, and meat. As the carts of food began to roll into camp, all rationing ceased. The internees could not remember having access to so much food. Although they could not eat a full meal without vomiting, they still, valiantly, tried.

Chinese pastors also arrived in camp. They reported, "how the Chinese church had been faring during the war years of ch'ih k'u (eating bitterness). Church attendance had dropped. . . . 'Rice Christians'[80] had fallen away, but a new quality of membership and leadership had emerged from the fires of trial and persecution." (Cliff, p. 119)

Besides food, the camp now had new clothing supplied by the Swiss Red Cross. The only problem was that it was Army issue. The men all walked around the camp wearing army khaki uniforms, military boots, and hats, while the children wore cut-off khaki uniforms. Even the women were forced to wear khaki dresses made out of the army uniforms as part of their clothing issue.

For the imbibers in camp, beer was readily available in the nearby villages, and they bartered for it using their allotted tins of milk powder and chocolate. After several years of abstinence, however, it didn't take much to induce intoxication. Meanwhile others went to church for Thanksgiving services.

---

[80] "Rice Christians" referred to the Chinese who expressed a belief in Jesus but did so for the benefit they felt it could bring them.

XXX

Homeward Bound

> 'Cause I've seen blue skies, through the tears
> In my eyes
> And I realize, I'm going home.[81]

Forty American military personnel were now running the camp, but the countryside was far from peaceful—rural Communists, Nationalist guerrillas, and bandit groups continued to fight fiercely around Weihsien. The Americans even paid the bandits a large sum of money for a ceasefire, but it was short lived.

The task at hand was to evacuate the camp and repatriate the internees to their respective countries. By mid-September arrangements were still being made. The task was daunting even though the camp now numbered approximately 1,500. As always, the numbers fluctuated: some had died, some had been born, and two had escaped. In September 1943, three hundred of the American internees were sent home, having been exchanged for Japanese prisoners of war. As well, a number of Catholic priests had left, transferred to an all-male internment camp when their superiors discovered that they had become too friendly with the women at Weihsien. Some priests had even been released earlier when the Pope declared them citizens of the Vatican, despite being from Allied countries.

Philip was going home. But Philip, like the other younger children, had difficulty understanding what "going home" meant. He did not know Canada; it was only a name. "School had been home, then Temple Hill and then Weihsien. Family was only a dim memory. . . . The people who loved them were their teachers and friends."[82]

---

[81] Song by Tim Curry, "I'm Going Home."
[82] Greenough, p. 34.

The first group scheduled to leave were the elderly and the infirm; they were followed by various other groupings. All of them needed to be transported to the town of Weihsien, and then to Tsingtao on the coast. They fixed September 24th as the departure date for the Chefoo group. Each packed his or her own luggage; Philip quickly packed his meagre belongings and a bit of parachute cord that he had managed to scrounge. Despite torrential rains that morning, the party of missionaries and children were loaded onto lorries and headed out. But the rains had turned the roads into quagmires, and they had to turn back. The next day, September 25th, the roads were in better condition and the group was successfully transported to Weihsien station, where they boarded the train for Tsingtao. They didn't leave a day too soon—the very next morning a band of guerrillas blew up the train tracks.

At Tsingtao, a crowd was waiting to greet them, and the American liberators of their country.

> In the crowd . . . was a Christian lady who had been an amah for many years at the Girls' School in Chefoo. She had wept as she watched (the children) being marched off into the concentration camp three years before. Now, with tears of joy streaming down her cheeks, she met staff and students again. She said "I had often seen (adults) going away, but never all those little ones. I have prayed for you every day, and now, surely, it is the Lord's grace to bring you out this way so that I can see how my prayers have been answered. My heart is satisfied." (Michell, pp. 142–143)

The contingent was put up at the Edgewater Mansions at Tsingtao—a grand hotel overlooking the China Sea. Philip had never enjoyed such luxury. The hotel had revolving doors and thick carpets on the floor. Philip had a gigantic room to himself, with a dresser for clothes, a real bed to sleep on with sheets and pillows, and water with which to wash that came out of a tap. He ate in a fancy dining room with a menu that contained every delicacy, and was served by Chinese waiters. He had his shoes shined and his bag carried by Japanese prisoners, and had money in his pocket, provided by the Swiss Red Cross. A party was even arranged for them aboard the British ship, the *H.M.S. Bermuda*.

From Tsingtao, Philip and the rest of his group were transported to Shanghai, where they boarded the troopship *U.S.S. La Vaca*. At Okinawa, the ship picked up 2,000 marines and carried on to San Francisco. One of the marines cut one of his uniforms down and sewed it to make a little outfit for Philip. On board this ship and others transporting the former Weihsien internees, the children and adults were shocked at the quality of food—cream, fruit, and bread made from finely sifted flour. However, much of it was too rich for their stomachs, which had become used to the Weihsien menu, and they could eat very little. They also could not believe the amount of waste as they watched full bins of unused bread, fruit, and vegetables dumped into the sea through the kitchen porthole.

Philip wrote a brief account of his arrival in North America. "In San Francisco we were placed under the care of the Red Cross. We were again fed properly for a few weeks, given more clothes, and finally placed on trains to return home."[83] The first stop was Vancouver, where Cliff's parents were waiting to meet Philip. Quickly his clothes were deloused and some of his belongings burnt because of bedbugs. Then he was back on the train. On November 11, 1945, after five years and three months without seeing or hearing from his parents, Philip arrived in Edmonton, Alberta. He was twelve years old, wearing a cut-down American Armed Forces uniform, speaking with a British accent and carrying a knapsack stuffed with parachute cord from Weihsien. Cliff was there to meet him. At first neither recognized the other, but then came the long-awaited warm embrace.

---

[83] *Young Pilot*, p. 31.

The Edmonton Journal.
Monday, November 12, 1945

Rev. Clifford T. Paulson, Three Hills, met his son Phillip, 12, Sunday night on the C.N.R. station platform here for the first time in five years and three months. At first neither father nor son recognized each other, as Phillip had been held by Japanese since the Chinese school he was attending was over-run before Pearl Harbor. Mr. Paulson, his wife and three other children fled their Chinese mission to the safety of India after the famous first Doolittle raid on Tokyo in 1942. The story of Mr. Paulson's part in aiding the daring American fliers when they crash-landed in China after the raid was told for the first time to THE EDMONTON JOURNAL.

Father Reunited With Son Freed From Jap Captivity

By Hal Pawson

Rev. Clifford Theodore Paulson, a tall, thin, fair man hustled down the C.N.R. platform Sunday night, his staring eyes searching for his son. Phillip Paulson, a small, thin, fair boy of 12, stood on the steps of an eastbound trans-continental train, his eyes searching for his father.

Father passed within four feet of son, and neither knew it—until an immediate woman relative recognized the bright neat boy as the nephew she had seen only as an infant. That brought father, a preacher and teacher at the Three Hills Prairie Bible school, and son, a prisoner of the Japanese in China since Pearl Harbor, together again for the first time in five years and three months.

It was a wordless reunion. It was a tearless reunion. Words and tears could not say what two smiles said when those two tumbled into each other's arms.

Those two smiles released an hitherto untold story of the Alberta missionary's part in the famous first raid on Tokyo by Gen. James Doolittle's American airmen on April 18, 1942.

The story of how Mr. Paulson played a human role in aiding American airmen returning from the raid, both dead and alive, remained until Sunday night a vital secret between the missionary and a few high Allied officials, Doolittle included. For on the story, told publicly for the first time to THE EDMONTON JOURNAL, balanced possible death of Phillip Paulson at the hands of the Japanese.

But let the history of the Paulsons, since Phillip was born in Innisfail in 1934, unfold itself in chronological order.

An infant of less than six months, Phillip left Innisfail with his parents for a mission in Kiangsi province, near Shangjao, in northern China. While there, Phillip's sister, Elaine, and two younger brothers, Keith and Blakely, were born. Only Elaine ever saw her brother as he was at school when the brothers were born.

Couldn't Reach Son

The school was the China Inland mission school, at Chefoo, Shantung province, several hundred miles from the Paulson's home mission. Before Pearl Harbor brought America and Canada to war with Japan, the Japanese overran Chefoo so suddenly that Mr. and Mrs. Paulson could not get their young son, then only six, out and to the safety of Kiangsi province in time.

"We weren't in a camp, but the Japanese guarded the school and kept us in there until Pearl Harbor," stated Phillip, matured, dignified, unabashed and well-mannered beyond his 12 years. "After Pearl Harbor they began taking over the school buildings one by one and we soon were moved to the North China camp at Weihsien."

"It was impossible to get through the Japanese lines to our boy," related Mr. Paulson. "Then in 1942 Gen. Doolittle raided Tokyo for the first time.

Americans Were Killed

"Many of the planes came back from Japan to Shangjao. The strips were not ready for them and most of the planes crashed attempting to land. Many American fliers were killed, others were hurt, and still others were dead as a result of the raid.

"I was the only white man in the entire district. Doolittle called me to his headquarters and for two days I was with him, arranging for the purchase of a burial field for the Americans, officiating at the many burial services and trying to gather the American dead.

"The Japanese found where the planes had landed and started a drive through Kiangsi province. They began overrunning Shangjao before I could complete my work. My family and I had to flee before their advance, leaving some American dead still lying along the roadsides.

Placed Son in Danger

"It was my duty to those Americans, yet it placed the life of my interned son in terrible jeopardy. Had the Japanese ever discovered my identity I believe my son would have been killed in reprisal. They knew a white man had helped the Americans, but this story was so well silenced that they never learned who that white man was. Now it does not matter. My son is home, safe and sound, thank God."

Knowing Phillip was a Japanese prisoner, the Paulsons were forced to flee before the advancing Japanese armies, through southern China, across Burma and into the safety of India. At the time of the long, perilous trek, Mr. Paulson was suffering from malaria, a malady which still strikes him periodically.

Mr. Paulson's ambition is to return to his missionary work in China. "If the way is ever cleared for me I shall return at once," he stated Sunday night.

Of his long internment by the Japanese, young Phillip said: "They did not treat us badly. The Chinese were more poorly treated. There were so many of them they could not be put in camps. We went to school all the time in camp, although we could not do as much as when we were in the mission school.

"Our happiest time was the day three days after the war ended that American planes dropped 250 parachutes of food to us and also dropped seven men—interpreters and such. From then until we started moving to Chindow and the boat that was taking us home they dropped food all the time. My, we ate like we hadn't for years.

"We used to get the news quickly. There was a Chinese who came in to clean the cesspools in the camp. He was a secret service man from Chungking and he gave us all the news. We knew as soon as the war was over. The people in the camp were all so happy that when the American planes came over we all ran out of the camp, and the Japs did not do anything.

Didn't Know Father

"I didn't know my father when I got here. I couldn't remember what he looked like. But it is posh to be home and see him again. I never saw my young brother Blakely before. Monday I will see mother and Elaine and Keith. It is so much. I also had a posh visit with my grandfather and grandmother (Mr. and Mrs. Benjamin Paulson) for two days in Vancouver.

"I didn't have any clothing when I started for home. We all came by boat, and when we stopped at Okinawa, a U.S. marine gave me an outfit. I had the little field cap, and they cut down the jacket and trousers. I got new clothing when we got to Los Angeles, but I'm keeping my marine suit. We were just out of Pearl Harbor on the boat when I had my 12th birthday."

Phillip was 1 1/2 months traveling from China to Vancouver. Only sad touch at the station Sunday night was when he said goodbye to his teacher, Miss Pearl Young, of Pictou, N.S., and nine other Canadian children.

Continued to Study

"Most of these children know no one but the people in the Weihsien camp," explained Miss Young. "I was their teacher at the inland mission school. The Japanese let us continue our studies, although the accommodations were poor. The food and sanitary facilities were poor, but there was no bad treatment. And the older people in the camp were good to the children. They even saw they had a better than fair share of the food. And they have been fed so well since we were liberated." Miss Young is conducting the party of nine children as far as Toronto. She will take her year's furlough at her home and then hopes to be allowed to return to China. When the party left China, there were 19 children from the school in it.

Mr. Paulson, Phillip and Blakely spent Sunday night at the Edmonton home of Mr. Paulson's sister, 11727 90 st. Monday, they left for Three Hills, where Phillip again will see his mother and meet his other brother and sister.

A dozen other relatives were at the C.N.R. station to greet him Sunday night. He cut a happily dignified figure in his short green heavy jacket and blue trousers as he formally acknowledged their acquaintance with handshakes and serious thoughtful answers to their questions.

Among those who greeted him was his 12-year-old cousin, Clifford Paulson, son of Mr. and Mrs. P. O. Paulson, 9111 88 ave. "Where did you get that English accent?" demanded Clifford in his hard Canadian drawl. "I was in an English school, you see," smiled back Phillip. "I'll have him talking Canadian in six months if I get the chance," Clifford stated later.

Appendix A

Genealogy

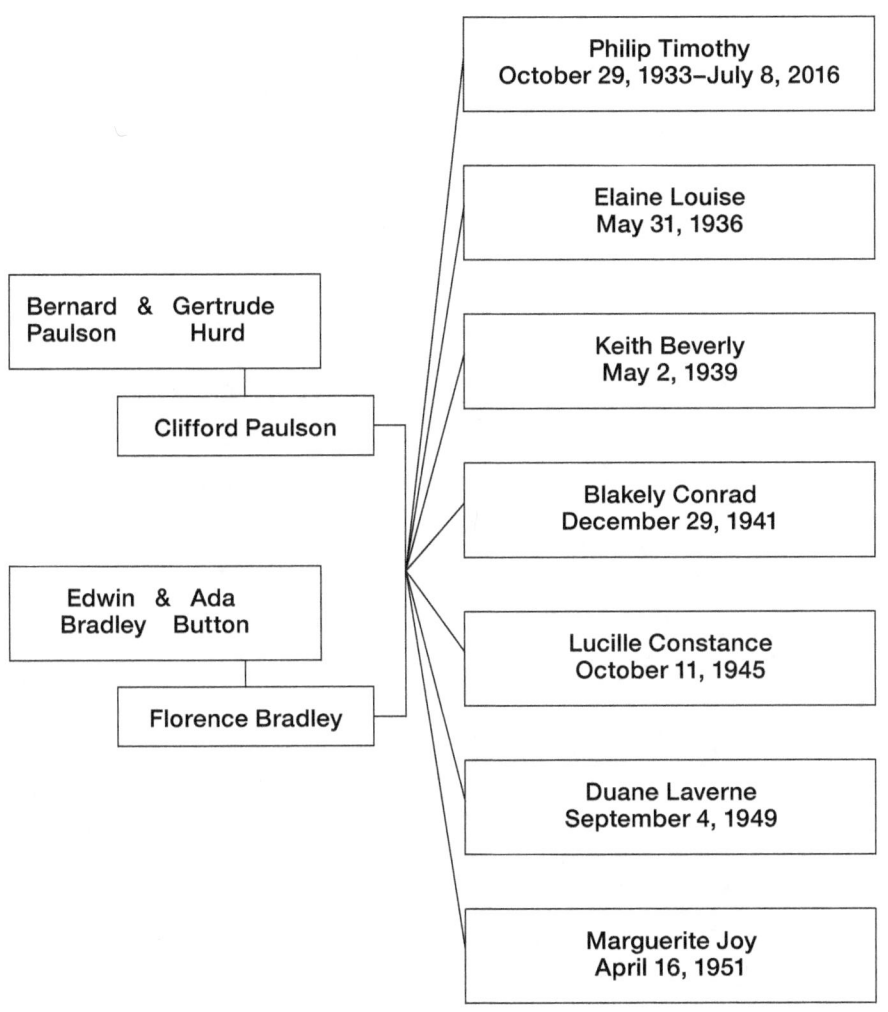

Appendix B

Clifford Theodore Paulson
May 5, 1907–November 26, 1986

Clifford's testimony as printed in *China's Millions*, November 1934[84]

"He . . . beheld . . . Levi, sitting at the place of toll, and said unto him, Follow me" —Luke 5:27, R.V.

But a few short years ago in the city of Calgary, Alberta, God in his mercy reconciled me to Himself by Jesus Christ. I had become conscious of the fact that I was a sinner with sins red like crimson, and therefore unprepared to meet the Lord Jesus who shall be revealed from heaven with his mighty angels, in flaming fire taking vengeance on them that know not God, and that obey not the gospel (2 Thessalonians 1:7, 8). I bowed before Him, accepted His pardon, and asked Him to wash my heart in His blood, which cleanses whiter than snow.

And now it is with gratitude and praise in my heart to Him that I have received from Him "the ministry of reconciliation" (2 Corinthians 5:18). He is sending me forth to other lost sheep "to open their eyes, and to turn them from darkness to light, and from the power of Satan unto God" (Acts 26:18).

Well do I remember those days in which He spoke to me through His Word about service in the vineyard. With the office door barred, thus shutting out the busy world, and with my little, red-covered Testament before me on the chair, I spent time each morning with God, listening to what He had to say. His grace alone enabled me, as it did Levi, to forsake all, rise up, and follow Him. Two years later my wife and I graduated from the Prairie Bible Institute at Three Hills, Alberta, at which institution I had learned to love God's Word more than ever.

I might say that the condition of the millions in the unreached regions, who are dying without the Saviour, and my consequent responsibility to those who "are carried away unto death, and those that are ready to be

---

[84] *China's Millions*, November 1934, p. 173.

slain" (Proverbs 24:11, R.V.) have rested heavily upon my heart ever since I was saved.

Hence I am pouring out my life to Him in love upon the altar of service, trusting that He will use it in winning back the precious souls for whom Christ died.

Clifford's autobiographical record, titled "Roots":

Someone has well said that it is just as important to "know where you came from" as to "know where you are going."

I was born May 5, 1907 on a farm near Bawlf, Alberta, in which town my father later bought and operated a hardware store. After a couple of years he sold the store at Bawlf, bought a hardware business at Cadogan and built a home. We were 5 children (one girl and four boys). I completed 8 grades at Cadogan Public School, took Grade 9 at Czar High School, grades 10, 11 & 12 at Provost High School, then attended Teachers Training College at Camrose where Florence and I first met and began our friendship.

Florence also was born on a farm near Olds, Alberta, June 18, 1908. Later the family (consisting of 1 boy & 3 girls) moved into the town of Olds, then on to Stettler, Alberta, where her father worked for the railroad and the children took their schooling (public and high school). Her father died at Stettler when she was 3 years old leaving the mother and the 4 children. After completing public and high school, Florence went on to Teachers Training College at Camrose and as I said previously, this is where we first met. She then taught at Black Hill, Gadsby, Buffalo Lake and Esther. I taught in 2 schools but decided to get other work as the winters were cold and the pay low, so I went into Edmonton where I worked as cashier at General Trust, then on to Calgary where the climate was warmer and got a job as a de-coder with California Fruit Growers Exchange (all business was done by secret code between California and the Calgary office). At that time Florence's sister, Frances, was married and living in Calgary so Florence visited her sister occasionally. It was in Calgary then that we met again and began to go together seriously. We attended the young peoples meetings and Sunday services at the Prophetic Bible Institute Church where Dr. Imrie was pastor.

Florence: A Missionary in China

We decided to be married at the parsonage on Saturday February 7th of that year, 1931, then went off to Banff by train for a weekend honeymoon. In Calgary we had rented a small upstairs suite in a private home at the corner of 6th Avenue and 8th Street S.W. which building incidentally was recently pulled down for high-rise development. While living there we came in contact with various missionaries who visited Calgary and felt called to offer ourselves for missionary service abroad. Accordingly I gave up my job and we vacated the little suite and left for Three Hills for Bible training to prepare for missionary work. Because of our age and educational qualifications we were able to take a 2 year crash course, graduating in the spring of 1933. We did pastoral work at Wimborne, Alberta, and were accepted as missionaries under the China Inland Mission. Our first child, Philip, was born 5 months after we graduated from Bible School and we left for China in the summer of 1934. Our days in China were difficult ones due mainly to the Japanese invasion. God gave us Elaine during this dark period, also Keith and Blake. The children of our mission school where Philip attended were interned for almost 4 years and we were unable to bring him back to Canada with us when we evacuated in 1944. Back in Canada I taught at Prairie Bible Institute for 7 years. Lucille, Duane and Marguerite were born during this time. After the teaching period at Three Hills I represented our Mission in Western Canada until 1971 when I officially retired. In closing I wish to pay tribute and give thanks to God for my faithful, capable helpmate, Florence, and our children who have been a great strength to me and my work. Proverbs 19:14 says "a prudent (this means sensible) wife is from the Lord" and Psalm 127:3 says "children are an heritage (this means gift) of the Lord." I thank the Lord for a practical helpful faithful wife and for our 7 wonderful children. They have made life worthwhile.

Can Souls Be Released Apart From Prayer?

Personal work class was in session at Prairie. The teacher was stressing the necessity of prayer if souls were to be born into the kingdom of God. "In fact," he declared, "I don't believe any soul that hasn't first been prayed for is ever saved."

A young man arose to his feet to challenge the statement. "I don't believe anyone ever prayed for me," he said, "my parents never did so and I don't know of anyone else who could have prayed for my salvation."

As we pondered his words a hush fell over the classroom. Could it be that no one had ever prayed for this young man? The question was unanswered, so we parted.

Four years passed and one day two Christian lady workers were visiting homes in a rural district. It was evening, and as they prayed that God would lead them to a home for the night where they could bring cheer and comfort to some needy soul, they drew up to a farm house and were given a hearty welcome by one of God's dear but lonely children. As the hours passed the conversation centred around Christ. Knowing they had come from Prairie the lady of the home suddenly asked, "Do you know Cliff Paulson?"

"Yes," answered the visitors, "he was in our class."

"And where is he now?" was the eager inquiry.

"He is in China."

"In China," exclaimed our most interested hostess as her eyes flooded with tears, "in China!"

She drew her chair more closely to us, wiped back her tears, looked into our puzzled faces and said, "Let me tell you a story."

"I was working in a city restaurant as cashier," she began, "when one day a tall thin young man came in for lunch. 'Pray for that young man,' whispered a voice within. 'But I don't know him,' I argued. I had never seen him before, but I bowed my head and prayed for him. The next day he appeared again and again the urge came to pray for his soul. For several days this continued until I longed to know more of this youth and to understand the Lord's strange promptings to pray."

"One night I attended a gospel service in the city and the preacher urged men and women to surrender their lives to God. As the call was given my soul suddenly bounded with joy when I saw this same young man rise to his feet and make his way to the front. Again I prayed earnestly for his salvation. Now I felt my curiosity must be satisfied. What was his name and did he really find the Lord? I remained behind and learned that his name was Cliff Paulson and he had truly found Christ as his Saviour."

Now was the visitors turn to magnify the Lord as they recalled that classroom some four years before and statement of this same young man, "I don't think anyone ever prayed for me." They rejoiced in the faithfulness of our God.

Christian, have you ever felt the Holy Spirits urge to pray for some one? Obey that voice; it is the voice of God. Pray as He directs and some day you too will understand.

Appendix C

China Inland Mission

The China Inland Mission (CIM) or as it is called in Chinese, Zhong Guo Nei Di Hui, was formally founded in 1865 in England by a physician, Dr. James Hudson Taylor. Its sole purpose was the evangelization of China, particularly the interior, which had not been reached by other missions.

The Mission was interdenominational in that its missionaries were drawn from various denominations—Baptist, Anglican, Methodist, as well as other Christian faiths. The only requirement of its candidates was their belief in a core set of principles, including the divine inspiration and authority of the Bible, the Trinity, man's nature of sin, atonement through the substitutionary death of Jesus, the resurrection, justification by faith, eternal life for the saved, and damnation for the unsaved. On other points they could differ. As to background, Florence had been raised Anglican while Cliff came from a non-Christian home.

The Mission had a non-solicitation—no debt policy, the cardinal rule being that financial need was to be mentioned to no one but God and no money was ever to be asked for, borrowed, or owed: God would provide. In paying their missionaries there was no set salary, only a division of whatever monies came in at the time. As stated in each issue of their magazine, *China's Millions*, "The Mission does not go into debt. It guarantees no income, but ministers to workers as funds sent in will allow. All members are expected to depend on God alone for temporal supplies. No collection or personal solicitation of money is authorized."[85] Cliff followed this principle throughout his life and never had a church offering taken whenever he preached. Female missionaries were accorded the same status, equality, and monies as the male missionaries.

Several regulations were set out for the missionaries. They were to live alongside the Chinese people, adopt Chinese names, eat Chinese food, and dress like the Chinese. Like other Chinese women, Florence wore a silk or padded gown, slit at the sides to just below the knee, with a mandarin collar, knotted buttons, and cloth shoes. Her hair was pulled back from her face and worn in

---

[85] Gardella, p. XIV.

a bun at the back, as the Mission did not allow women to have short hair. The missionaries were to act as evangelists, teachers, and servants to the Chinese.

Appendix D

Chiang Kai-shek's Conversion to Christianity[86]

Although obviously never destined to really govern China, he united the country and supported the missionaries as a Christian, opening a brief window for the evangelism of China before the door was closed by the Communists.

Chiang Kai-shek had a long-time association with the Soong family, a very wealthy and influential Christian family in China. The elder Soongs had made their fortune publishing and selling Chinese Bibles and other Christian literature. Sun Yat-Sen had been married to one of their daughters, Chingling, and Chiang was interested in marrying their third daughter, Mayling, who had been educated in the United States.

In 1927, Chiang met with Mrs. Soong, who was living at that time in Japan, to ask for Mayling's hand in marriage. As a protective mother, Mrs. Soong had concerns with Chiang's Buddhist background and was reluctant to give her consent to the marriage.

> Mrs. Soong said that she understood Chiang was not a Christian; was he willing to become one? At that point the aspiring son-in-law won her heart. Instead of protesting hastily that of course he would be a Christian, or anything else that pleased her, he replied slowly that he would look into the matter. He would read the Bible and see what there was in it. He was perfectly willing to try. . . . Mrs. Soong was impressed by the General's honesty,

and gave her consent for the marriage.[87] On December 1, 1927, Chiang and Mayling were married in a private religious ceremony in the Soong home, followed by a large Chinese wedding.

---

[86] Although there has always been some scepticism as to Chiang Kai-shek's actual conversion in that his government in China was known for its corruption, graft, and ruthless oppression of its opponents, Chiang himself was considered personally honest. He read his Bible and prayed every day and, like King David, said, ". . . it was in my mind to build an house unto the name of the Lord my God: But the word of the Lord came to me, saying, thou hast shed blood abundantly, and hast made great wars: thou shalt not build an house unto my name, because thou hast shed much blood upon the earth in my sight." (1 Chronicles 22:7–8)

[87] Hahn, p. 123.

In discussing his view of Christians, Chiang had made a comment to his wife, saying,

> I can't understand these Christians; why, they have been treated most abominably here, they have been robbed, beaten, many of them killed, they have been persecuted fearfully, and yet I never find one of them retaliating, and any time they can do anything for China, for our people, they are ready to do it; I do not understand them. Mayling replied, "Well that, you see, is the very essence of Christianity. They do that because they are Christians."[88]

True to his word, Chiang took time out of every day to read the Bible. Mayling anxiously awaited his decision. Once, when becoming impatient, she telegraphed the Reverend Kiang in Shanghai, asking him to come and talk to her husband as she felt that he was just about ready to become a Christian. Although both of them talked to him while driving in a motorcade, with bodyguards riding ahead and more bodyguards behind, Chiang refused to be rushed. "'I have just finished reading the New Testament for the second time,' he said, 'and am now going to begin to read the Old Testament. I want to learn more about this Christian faith before I publicly accept Jesus Christ as my Savior.'" (Hahn, p. 130)

Finally, Chiang was ready to commit himself and so informed Reverend Kiang.

> For one thing, he said, Christian officers seemed to fight better than others . . . . Moreover, Chiang had undergone a crisis during a crucial battle near Kaifeng when he found himself in danger of being cut off from his troops.
>
> "In this desperate situation, he prayed to God for deliverance, pledging that he would publicly acknowledge Jesus Christ as his Lord after the Lord had delivered him," the pastor reported. "God did answer his prayer by sending a very heavy snowstorm, which was unusual at this time of year, so that his enemies could not advance any nearer. In the meantime, his reinforcements came from Nanking by rail, thereby not only sparing his own life, but turning a certain defeat into a victory."

---

[88] J. Vernon McGee, *Thru The Bible*, 1 Corinthians through Revelation, p. 809.

Florence: A Missionary in China

> One side of the bargain having been fulfilled, Chiang in the approved Old Testament manner kept his word too, and Pastor Kiang duly baptized him. (Hahn, p. 147)

After becoming a Christian, Chiang joined the Southern Methodist Church. Faithfully he read his Bible every morning, and when in 1936 some of his troops mutinied and he was taken prisoner, the only thing he asked for was his Bible. During his capture, Madame Chiang held off his enemies in Nanking, who wanted him executed. Later, when she went to his aid and Chiang saw his wife, he wrote, "'I was very much moved and almost wanted to cry.' He declared that he had read in the Bible only that morning, 'Jehovah will now do a new thing, and that is: He will make a woman protect a man.'" (Hahn, p. 211)

Appendix E

Alfred Bosshardt and Arnolis Hayman

In the early 1930s, the province of Kiangsi was a stronghold for Communist activity. Numerous battles were fought between the Nationalist soldiers under Chiang Kai-shek and the Communist or Red Armies, and numerous cities and towns were taken and lost by each army, with upheaval for everyone. In the late 1920s and early 1930s, the death toll in Kiangsi Province alone was seven million people. Christians were marked for particular cruelty and death, with the Communists viewing missionaries as Imperialist spies or government agents who camouflaged their motives by propagating religion.

In 1934, the situation settled down when Communist leaders called a retreat of their armies after losing several major battles. The intent was to regroup in northwest China. There they were to reorganize and retrain for further combat. Starting out from Kiangsi, the scattered troops commenced their formidable trek, which became known as the Long March.[89] It covered 6,000 miles and traversed through six provinces. An estimated 100,000 men and women participated in the journey, but only one out of ten survived. Among the survivors were most of the generals, other military officers, and Communist leaders who had ridden horses and probably ate better than the troops.

Although the Long March initially headed for the province of Shansi, the warlord there, Yen Hsi-shan, threatened by such a large military band of refugees, routed them toward Shensi. There, in the primitive walled city of Yenan, the march ended. Yenan, a city of about 500,000 inhabitants, was situated on one of the camel caravan routes leading to inner Mongolia and north China. Outside the city were hundreds of caves in which the Communists set up their headquarters and dwellings.

During the march, several CIM missionaries were taken captive. One was Alfred Bosshardt, who later wrote a book about his ordeal called *The Guiding Hand*. Alfred and his wife, Rose, had been attending a prayer conference at Anshun. When returning to their home at Chenyuan in Kweichow Province

---

[89] There were actually several long marches under different generals or Communist leaders.

they were taken prisoner by Communist soldiers. It was October 1934. The couple and their entourage, which included their cook, another Chinese Christian, and four porters who had been carrying Rose's sedan chair, were marched to Kuichow. Three additional missionaries were rounded up: Arnolis and Rhoda Hayman and their two young children, and Grace Emblen. A ransom of 700,000 silver dollars was set for the foreigners, 100,000 dollars apiece, and they were instructed to write the Mission and their consuls for the funds. The next day, the four Chinese porters were released and shortly thereafter the wives and children, although the ransom remained the same. Rose and Rhoda attempted to telegraph the Mission of the happenings but were unable to do so immediately as the young manager at the telegraph office had been beaten to death and his father taken prisoner.

At the end of the second day of captivity, Alfred was summoned by one of the Communist Generals, General Xiao Ke. He had acquired a detailed map of Kweichow Province, likely taken from a Roman Catholic mission, and wanted the locations translated into Chinese. The map was in French, a language that Alfred had learned earlier so as to better communicate with his wife's French-speaking family. Alfred hesitated at the request but, remembering Jesus' command to "love your enemies, do good to those who hate you, bless those who curse you, pray for those who ill-treat you," translated the map. The general was extremely grateful as he had been leading his men blindly through the province, relying on crude, inadequate maps found in school textbooks. Now he could plan a strategic route, avoiding government strongholds, and head in the direction he needed to go.

The pace of the march was gruelling for the missionaries, sometimes travelling forty miles a day. Alfred and Arnolis were worried for Grace, and afraid that she would not be able to stand the ordeal. One day, when Grace was at the end of her strength and lagging behind, she heard an inner voice prompting her to "stand still and see the salvation of the Lord, which he will show you today." So she stood in her tracks. After a while she got tired of standing so she sat on a stone and watched as all of the soldiers walked by her and gradually disappeared into the distance. From there, she and the Bosshardt's Chinese cook, who had been helping her, made their way to Chenyuan.

Alfred and Arnolis were now the sole foreign prisoners of the Red Army. As they marched they sang hymns and prayed for their captors, other prisoners, their families, colleagues, and themselves, including the strength "to carry on." At night they read their Chinese Bible, counted their blessings for the day, and testified to the guards and other prisoners.

An ironic source of encouragement came when they were told to march behind the flag-bearer. Generally the communist flag—a bright red rectangle inset with a black star surrounding a hammer and sickle—would be unfurled and flown when going into battle or entering a village. At other times it was kept rolled up and wrapped in canvas. Alfred noticed that the canvas wrapping was actually a waterproof oil painting of Christ's birth, which he believed had been taken from the Gospel Hall at Pensui. The painting depicted the Nativity shepherds, their sheep, and the Star of Bethlehem. "And so," Alfred later recalled, "we followed the Christmas star. Like the wise men, uncertain where it would finally lead us!"[90] But most of all it was seen as a secret sign from God reassuring them of "His guiding hand."

As the march continued, difficulties mounted as the men had to survive both the intense heat of summer and the cold of winter, with few clothes and straw sandals that quickly wore out. There were rugged, boulder-strewn mountains to cross, where sleeping on the slopes meant not turning over in the night for fear of falling to one's death. They waded knee deep in icy streams and crossed deep rivers and ravines on hastily improvised bridges made from doors and tables. On the roadways lay the rotting corpses of men executed by the Red Army. At night they heard screams and pleadings of prisoners being tortured and people being led out for beheading. Once Alfred and Arnolis were beaten with a long notched bamboo switch after they attempted to escape. Although gone for several days, twice they circled back on themselves before they were recaptured close to their starting point.

At the end of "a day's march," which could last two days and a night without resting, there would sometimes be a meagre meal consisting of mouldy rice, or even no meal at all. One night the soldiers had confiscated an ox that they killed and cut up for food. The next morning a soldier handed Alfred and Arnolis a bowl of sliced raw meat. All day they carried their precious commodity and cooked it for supper, only to discover the next day that the soldier had only meant for them to carry it for him, not eat it.

---

[90] Bosshardt, p. 86.

When extolling the virtues of the Communists, many writers have emphasized that, wherever they went, Communist soldiers always paid the peasants for everything they used, be it food, lodging, or equipment that they had borrowed. The truth of the matter is that they paid for these things with what they had stolen from everyone else. Alfred commented on this situation, noting that after

> the home of a wealthy landowner was taken over . . . true to form, the comrades appropriated whatever they wanted of the man's goods and called on the local peasants to help themselves to his stocks of grain. Watching this, Alfred asked a comrade, "where do you draw the line between peasant and landowner?" The reply was, "If someone tills his own soil, he's all right. If others work his land, he's an oppressor." Thanks to this particular oppressor, the Red Army was able to feast on pork, duck and chicken.[91]

Arnolis Hayman, in his account of his captivity during the Long March, went on to describe a hierarchy to the division of looting: "According to Hayman, the senior officials seized any valuables, while ordinary soldiers were given a licence to take anything else they found for their own personal needs. . . . The poor people got only what was left over."[92] Landowners, merchants, usurers, foreign missionaries, and Chinese Christians were particular targets for looting. Typically when a landowner was killed, his property was given to the peasants who had joined the Red Army, thus, making them the "new landowner." Later, even the peasants, who had been given some land from the liquidated rich, had their land taken away and were themselves killed.

During the march, the Communists held regular indoctrination sessions during which political lectures were given and Communist songs sung. "Hayman was particularly disturbed by the fact that one of the most popular songs in the Red Army 'Kill, kill, kill, let the whole world run with blood' was sung to the tune of a well-known Christian song, 'Jesus Loves The Little Children.'" (Brady, p. xxiii)

To help pass the time at night Alfred obtained some wool. His mother had taught him to crochet as a child, and he made a crochet hook out of the sharpened end of a chopstick and started making various woollen items. First

---

[91] Bosshardt, p. 79.
[92] Hayman, p. xx.

he made a pair of bed socks for Arnolis, then a cap for the army trumpeter. After that, orders from army officials and soldiers poured in, and he was kept busy, keeping boredom away while filling any free time he had.

After a year in captivity, a friend of the Mission paid 10,000 silver dollars for the release of the prisoners. The money weighed four hundred pounds and required four porters to carry it. Although both Alfred and Arnolis had been promised their freedom, the Communists failed to keep their end of the agreement and only released Arnolis. By that time he had spent 413 days in captivity, was unable to walk, and barely weighed one hundred pounds. A sedan chair was provided for him in which to ride. Quickly the group that had brought the money left, along with Arnolis, travelling to Yongshun and then Yuanling. Just as they left Yuanling, the Communists returned, intending to recapture Arnolis and hold him for ransom again. They missed him by only a few minutes.[93]

Six months later and after 560 days in captivity, Alfred was released. It was Easter Sunday, April 12, 1936. He was put on bed rest for eleven weeks as he was found to be suffering from pleurisy, bronchitis, beri-beri and sprue, but he was free.

---

[93] Arnolis' days of captivity were not over. Later, he and his wife were interned by the Japanese and separated from three of their children who were interned with Philip at Weihsien.

Appendix F

Boxer Uprising

In the thirty-five years that followed its founding, the CIM lost only one of its members to violence.[94] Then in 1900 the Mission lost fifty-eight missionaries along with twenty-one of their children. Of all the missionary societies operating in China, the CIM suffered the greatest loss of life.

This deathblow was dealt by a loosely organized society of Chinese called Boxers. Originating in northern China, various bands of men would travel through villages and rural areas exciting the people to riot, loot, and kill all foreigners including missionaries and adherents of the foreign religion. Similar societies were not unusual in China, being formed by villagers for self-protection to ward off bandits and protect themselves from unscrupulous landlords. The Boxers were different, however, in that they were not formed for self-protection but were the actual perpetrators and instigators of violence. Their battle cries were "Sha! Sha!"—"Kill! Kill!"—and "Sha kuei tsz"—"Kill the devils." They carried banners and posted handbills in the villages with the words "Meih Yang"—"Exterminate Foreigners." At first they were tolerated by the Chinese authorities, then utilized by them, and in the end were actually directed by the Imperial Palace and Empress Dowager.

In June of 1900, the Imperial Palace issued an edict that was telegraphed throughout China. It read, "Feng yang-jen pi sha, yang-jen t'ui hui chi sha"—"The foreigners must be killed, even if the foreigners leave, they must still be killed." Likely there would have been more deaths resulting from this edict except for two Chinese ministers, Hsu Ching Ch'eng and Yan Ch'ang, who substituted the word "pao"—"to protect"—for the word "sha"—"to kill." The edict now read, "The foreigners must be protected, even if the foreigners leave, they must still be protected." For their humane act, the ministers were executed.

---

[94] On November 4, 1898, several men attacked William Fleming and his native evangelist, P'an, while travelling in Kweichow Province. One of the men slashed the evangelist with his sword, and Mr. Fleming dismounted the mule he was riding to help his friend. Both were put to death.

The actual Chinese name for the Boxers was I Ho Chu'an, meaning "Fists of Public Harmony," with the word fists (chu'an) being a reference to boxing. They were well trained in martial arts and typically dressed in red, with a red cloth around their heads and a red sash around their waists.

Prior to fighting, they would engage in a specific ritual in which they prostrated themselves and invoked specific incantations or chants while facing pictures of various deities, inviting the spirit of their particular god to possess and assist them. A trance followed, characterized by bodily contortions, foam spewing from the mouth, and eyes rolling back in the head, after which they would fall to the ground and then jump up again quickly, prepared to fight. At this point they were considered impervious to swords and spears, and even bullets.

Most Chinese people, and even the Chinese Christians, believed the Boxers' claims of invincibility, and any sceptics were quickly silenced. When an Imperial official informed the Empress Dowager that he had actually seen Boxers dead in the field, riddled with bullet holes, the Empress sharply reprimanded him, stating that he must be mistaken and that the bodies he saw could not possibly be those of Boxers but of outlaws instead.

While it was the Boxers who brought death to the foreigner and destruction of their property, it could have been any number of factions within China at the time, given the anti-foreign sentiments of the Chinese government and the people. Conflict was inevitable. As a whole, the Chinese were embittered with the Western powers and their progressive encroachment on Chinese land and partition of the country into their own national territories. Several wars had preceded 1900, all of which ended with more concessions and territory lost to the West. Britain, France, Germany, Russia, and Japan all held territories they'd wrestled from the Chinese. From the Chinese point of view, the foreigners were seizing the country piece by piece, and if their territorial greed was not stopped there would be nothing left to save from their clutches. The Chinese were angry.

Along with the loss of territory came various concessions for telegraph lines, railways, and mining rights. The sale of land involved in these concessions was often compulsory and there was no regard for familial lines of property ownership. Nor was there regard for the sacred ancestral worship and gravesites that dotted the countryside. The Chinese peasants were highly superstitious. They believed that the telegraph poles that ran parallel with the railway tracks, which they referred to as "iron centipedes," were strung with the tongues of murdered children. When the wind blew they could hear the children moaning, and when it rained, they thought they could see their blood dripping down the poles, not understanding that it was just rust-coloured rainwater dripping from the deoxidized wires. The railways also destroyed the livelihood of boat and cart men who had previously made their living transporting goods on China's waterways and roads. The Chinese were unforgiving and only grew angrier. The first places destroyed during the Boxer uprising were railway lines and telegraph offices.

The West also brought machine-made goods to China, including factory-produced fabrics and enamel ware, which displaced existing cottage industries and resulted in artisans who could no longer make a living with their hand-weaving and pottery-making skills. Individuals, whole villages, the very ancient order of life were all disrupted.

Opium was another concern. Although foreigners did not introduce opium to China, they certainly expanded its sale and forced its legalization, against the wishes of the Chinese. Though opium was outlawed in Britain, the British forced the sale of it in China. Opium was bought from India, which put the Chinese growers out of business, and then sold to China in exchange for their silver, tea, silk, and porcelain. By 1900, it was estimated there were up to 40 million Chinese using opium, 15 million of whom were addicted to the drug. When China tried to halt the opium trade and protect its silver reserves, Britain entangled them in the Opium War that lasted from 1839 to 1842. In defeat, China was forced to open five new treaty ports in which foreigners could trade. China also ceded extraterritorial rights, allowing foreigners to govern themselves without interference from the Chinese government.

The foreign presence in China was established for trade and economic purposes. Traders, in fact, were not highly regarded by the Chinese, who valued scholars most and traders and military men least. The Chinese were not interested in travelling "the seas" and actually had a mistrust of water. They could not understand the persistent restlessness of foreign merchants which compelled them to come in large numbers to the Chinese coast. Arthur Smith, an American missionary with twenty-nine years of experience in China, wrote:

> The only explanation credible, or indeed conceivable, to the Chinese was
> the theory that the foreigner came because he was compelled to do so.

> He dwelt in a remote, circumscribed, unproductive, and impoverished corner of the earth, which produced neither tea-leaves nor rhubarb. Without tea he would have nothing to drink. Without rhubarb he was absolutely unable to digest his food. Commerce with China was to him, therefore, a condition of existence . . .[95]

To the Chinese, all foreigners were "yang kuei tsz"—foreign devils, or barbarians. Foreigners were looked down upon—the Chinese saw themselves as superior with respect to their history, culture, and civilization. They were insulated and self-sufficient, and did not feel the need or desire for anything the West had to offer.

Missionaries were also foreigners with new ideas and a new religion they wished to market in China. For the most part, the Chinese did not appear to have a real problem with the Christian message; they were quite tolerant of various religions and were themselves Buddhists, Taoists, or Confucians, and lived amicably alongside Muslims. What antagonized the Chinese was the Christian's rejection of ancestor worship, which was a mainstay of all their religious beliefs. The Chinese believed that each person was an inseparable and vital link in a long line of ancestors, and that the souls of the dead lived on in the natural world. By praying and making offerings to the spirits of dead relatives, their descendants could gain favour for themselves, influence their future and fortune, and perpetuate life itself. Thus, if a Chinese became a Christian and discontinued the practice of ancestor worship, the ancestral line would be broken and the whole family jeopardized. Furthermore, converted Chinese no longer contributed to religious festivals and theatricals, which typically was a village expense. Now, other members of the community had to pick up the remaining costs, thus creating intense hostility toward the Chinese convert. In showing their contempt, the Chinese referred to the Chinese Christian as "erh mao tsz," meaning "secondary devils," and no longer considered them to be Chinese.

Of all the missionary groups, the Chinese appeared to hold particular dislike for the Roman Catholics because of their interference in political and judicial matters on behalf of their converts. When a Protestant missionary was approached by a convert on a legal matter, the likely response was, "Let's pray about it"; but if a Catholic priest was approached, he would take the

---

[95] *China in Convulsion*, p. 10.

matter up with the local official and encourage a favourable verdict for his parishioner, whether the parishioner was in the right or the wrong. If that line of influence failed, the priest might make an appeal for justice to the French Consul, claiming a case of persecution. Consequently, the Roman Catholic converts were both feared and hated.

For years the Chinese Roman Catholic Church had attempted to attain official political status. On March 15, 1899, after years of pressure from France on behalf of the Church, an edict was issued from the Chinese government granting official rank to each level in the Roman hierarchy—bishops could adopt the same rank as a Chinese governor, a priest the rank of a magistrate, and so forth. Although the same rights were accorded the Protestant denominations, they universally refused.

A second reason Catholics were disliked was their acquisition of huge amounts of property. In fact, the Roman Catholic Church was at one point one of the largest foreign property owners in China. Typically, the Chinese were reluctant to sell land to foreigners and, most frequently, would only rent to them. In times of famine, the Roman Catholic Church would make small loans to farmers under certain conditions: attendance at religious services, studying the catechism, and mortgaging their land to the Church alongside annual grain taxes. If the loan could not be repaid in a specified time period, the Church would take the land. The Church also acquired land via the rights of land ownership granted to foreigners through various treaties.

A third reason Roman Catholics were disliked was their operation of orphanages. The Chinese abandoned or killed their children if they did not want or could not feed or look after them. This was an accepted practice. As such, the Chinese could not understand priests taking in large numbers of infants and children if it was not for the purpose of killing them and using their body parts for nefarious purposes. This belief was further corroborated by the revelation that children were being kept behind locked doors, with no one allowed to see or visit them. Then there was the strange practice of "last rites," or "pronouncing strange incantations" over dying children. Additionally confusing to the Chinese were: the Catholic practice of not opening their chapels to outsiders as other religious groups did, not conducting any medical work to speak of, and remaining in relative seclusion.

Despite everything else, the actual precipitating factor in the Boxer uprising and the violence it engendered was the drought of the summer of

1899, which continued unabated into the fall, and then over the winter and into the new year. Because of this circumstance, the fall crops failed and wheat, usually sown in the winter for spring harvest, could not be planted as the ground was too hard. With the drought came famine, and with the famine came starvation, with thousands upon thousands facing certain death. The people were fearful and discontented. Instead of being busily engaged on their farms, they were idle and hungry—they blamed the Christians for annoying the Chinese gods with their foreign religion and thus causing the drought. Then the violence started.

The first actual martyrdom occurred on the eve of 1900. The victim was Sidney Brooks, a twenty-four-year-old member of the Society for the Propagation of the Gospel. He had spent the Christmas holiday in Tsinan in the province of Hopei with his sister and was returning to his post in Shantung Province. During the holidays he'd experienced a disturbing dream. He dreamed that he was back in England, walking through his college, and saw a plaque on a wall bearing the names of all those who had gone from the school as missionaries. Next to it was another plaque with the inscription, "To those who were martyred for the faith," and on it was his name. As Mr. Brooks was travelling, he was attacked by a group of Boxers who brutally beat him, stripped him, strung a rope through a hole they made in his nose, and mercilessly dragged him around for hours. Eventually he was able to free himself and tried to escape, but they hacked him to death with their swords and threw his body in a ditch.

Although Mr. Brooks was the first martyr of 1900, the initial thrust of violence committed by the Boxers was against Chinese Christians. Their homes were burned and they and their families, whether or not they too were Christian, were massacred. Some were burned alive, some were buried alive, some were thrown into wells, and some were slashed to pieces with swords. Others were tortured and had their noses and ears cut off and their eyes gouged out. The Boxers were often astonished by the demeanour and courage of the Christians when being tortured or facing death, and would cut their hearts out to see what gave them such inner peace.

In pillaging the missionary chapels and compounds, the Boxers actively sought out church registers so as to identify all Christians in the area and systematically seek them out for death. Virtually anyone associated with the missionaries became victims—converts, friends, servants, and even Chinese

Florence: A Missionary in China

who had visited the missionary hospitals and dispensaries. In some cases missionaries had the foresight to destroy their records. Most of the initial violence was perpetrated on the Protestant converts as the Roman Catholic converts were well protected in their fortified and armed compounds, although there were several instances of Roman Catholic congregations being burned alive in their cathedrals.

As the converts were being hunted and murdered, the missionaries also came under attack. Of those who died, some were burned alive while others were executed by beheading. The deaths by fire were particularly poignant.

In one instance, on June 30, 1900, the compound of the American Board Mission was set on fire. "As flames and smoke bellowed up, (one of the missionaries) May Simcox rushed from the front door with her baby Margaret in her arms. She begged the Boxers to spare the child, but they pushed her and the girl back inside." Upstairs, her husband, Frank Simcox, could be seen "walking to and fro by a window ... hand in hand with his two sons as flames engulfed" them.[96] All perished in the fire.

In another instance, Edith Coombs, of the same Mission, perished on June 27th when the premises in which she was living and working were set on fire. Initially she had escaped through the burning front gate of the compound, but returned inside when she realized that two young Chinese girls attending school there had not escaped with her. She found one of the girls and carried her outside and then went back in for the second girl. Finding her, she proceeded out the gate again, but on her way out she stumbled and fell. The crowd outside the premises started throwing bricks at the two of them.

> ... then a man rushed up and struck Coombs over the head. Coombs covered (the girl) with her body and whispered into her ear, "Don't be afraid; we shall soon be where there is no more pain and sorrow. We shall soon see Jesus."
>
> Coombs rose to her feet and begged the crowd to spare the girl's life. . . . Several men then seized Coombs and threw her on the bonfire. She managed to get up from the burning pile, but they shoved her back on it. She staggered to her feet again, walked a few steps, then knelt and started to pray. "See, she is pleading for her life," someone called out. "It is no good." Coombs was thrown back on the flames. People

---

[96] *Massacre in Shansi*, p. 208.

piled a door, tables and boards on top of her so she couldn't move. They watched as she burned to death.[97]

Other missionaries were beheaded. In the city of Tai Yuan in Shansi Province, Governor Yu Hsien, who had a hatred of foreigners, rounded up all the missionaries and Catholics living in the city and had them brought to his yamen, or compound. There they were stripped to the waist, as was the custom with condemned criminals about to be beheaded. Each prisoner knelt in turn in front of the executioner who, wielding a large sword, severed their heads. The men were beheaded first. At the time of death, some of the men were praying, some were talking to their captors about God, and some were calmly kneeling, waiting for the executioner's blow. Next to meet death were the women and children, with the mothers often holding the hand of their child, even after their deaths. After the Protestant missionaries came the execution of the Roman Catholic priests and Sisters of Mercy. Last were the Chinese converts. Those who witnessed the event remarked on the serenity of the foreigners, none of who cried out or made any noise, save two or three of the children. In that one day alone, July 9, 1900, thirty-three Protestant missionaries including their families and twelve Roman Catholics were killed, as well as a number of Chinese converts.

It was evening before the bloody task was finished. During the night, looters stripped the bodies left lying in the courtyard exactly where they fell of their remaining clothing, rings, and watches. The next morning, some of the heads were affixed to poles at the yamen, while others were placed in bamboo cages and hung from each of the city's four gates. The bodies were disposed of separately, thrown outside the city walls for the dogs to ravage. It was important to the Chinese that the bodies and the heads be separated after death, as they believed a person could not rest in peace in the afterlife unless his body was intact. They also believed that the Christians, if killed, would rise from the dead in three days unless the body was dismembered, burned, or left unburied.

Then there were the trials of those missionaries who'd attempted to escape, although many of them, and their children, died on their journey to safety, being beaten and stoned in the villages they passed through, suffering from lack of food and water, and being deprived of sleep. What little money or

---

[97] Ibid., p. 227.

Florence: A Missionary in China

possessions they had with them were stolen, and the only clothing they had was what was left on their backs. Sometimes even that was taken. Arthur Smith noted in his book, *China in Convulsion*, "On more than one occasion a missionary was deprived of every stitch of clothing, standing naked upon the streets of the inhospitable villages of Shansi" (p. 617). The deaths and suffering were even more horrific. A Ms. Rice, in her flight from Lu-ch'eng in Shansi, was beaten to death on the roadside, and a Ms. Huston was run over with a horse and cart in an attempt to break her spine, and then wounded so severely in the head that her brain was exposed. She died a month later, two days before reaching safety.

Those children who were old enough to understand compared it to how Jesus was treated, and spoke about the naughty soldiers who treated Jesus badly. China Inland Mission missionaries, Mr. and Mrs. Saunders' little Jessie, aged seven, who died on the road when they were stoned and beaten, said, "They treated Jesus like this, didn't they, Mother?"[98]

Some of the missionaries were actually captured by Boxers during their flight. Often they were taken to Boxer shrines where the spirits would decide when, where, and how they should die. Candles were lit and the drift of the smoke would determine their fate. Miraculously, a number of the missionaries were released.

Other Christians were caught and tortured before death. Bishop Hamer, who had spent over twenty years in China, was seized while celebrating Mass, bound, and marched through the city to be mocked. His hands were cut off while he scrolled through his rosary beads. Three days later he was stripped of his robes, wrapped in cotton, doused with gasoline and burned alive. Five thousand Catholic converts were killed, and every church and building in his diocese was destroyed.

During the Boxer uprising, the greatest loss of life among foreigners throughout northern China was suffered by Protestant missionaries. Of their number, 136 adults and fifty-three children were killed—84 percent of them in either Shansi or adjacent parts of Mongolia. In turn, the Roman Catholics lost forty-seven adults. Although the Catholics were more disliked by the Chinese, their compounds were usually sturdily built and heavily fortified, and both their priests and laypersons were often armed. They did, however,

---

[98] *Martyred Missionaries of the China Inland Mission*, p. 21.

suffer the greatest loss of converts. Approximately 30,000 Catholic converts were killed, likely a result of unfairly settled lawsuits through the priests. The number of Protestant converts who died was estimated to be about 1,900.

Who were these missionaries, as people, living in a foreign land? Arthur Smith answers this question, stating,

> They were earnest God-fearing men and women who had left all to obey the command of their Master to make known the glad tidings of the Kingdom of Heaven, men and women of irreproachable character and blameless lives; some of them graduates of the best colleges and universities, to whom attractive careers had been opened in their home lands, but upon which they turned their backs. Many of them had given long years of toil to the relieving of Chinese suffering in dispensary and hospital work."[99]

And some, who came from wealthy homes, even paid for it all with their own monies.

Perhaps better known in secular history is the Boxer attack on the Legations, the foreign settlements in Peking. In June of 1900, the Imperial Court declared that all foreigners were to leave China or be killed. In essence, war had been declared on them. On June 20th, the Legations, which included the embassies of Britain, France, and Japan, amongst others, were attacked by Imperial troops and the Boxers. By then, the missionaries and other foreigners living in and around Peking had retreated to the Legations and commenced preparations for the assaulting forces. The British Legation became the command post and Sir Claude MacDonald the overall commander. In Peking, every premise belonging to or formerly occupied by foreigners, including hospitals and schools, was looted and burned. Even the foreign cemeteries were desecrated and a number of the bodies dug up, their bones used for bonfires.

The first concentrated attack by the Chinese was against the Northern Cathedral of the Roman Catholic Church, or Pei T'ang, which was defended from June 15th until August 16th. During the siege, the cathedral housed seventy-three foreigners, forty of whom were French and Italian marines, who had been sent from the Legations to defend the cathedral, as well as 3,200 Chinese converts.

---

[99] *China in Convulsion*, p. 618.

Florence: A Missionary in China

The marines had only one rifle each and a canon that they had captured from the Chinese. The cathedral was completely isolated during the siege and there were no messages in or out. They had few provisions and, near the end of the siege, were barely subsisting on chaff, grass, and leaves of trees. Ten foreigners were killed in the siege, as were numerous Chinese converts.

A second Roman Catholic cathedral in Peking, known as the South Cathedral, was burned and hundreds of Chinese converts who had sought refuge there were killed. Those who survived escaped to the Legations. Initially the converts were refused entrance as authorities felt they needed all of their resources for themselves. Eventually they were admitted through the assistance and insistence of their Catholic leaders. As fortune would have it, across from the British Legation was the palace of Prince Su, a Manchurian official who had vacated his premises. His palace and grounds thus became part of the defended area and were used to house the Catholic converts. It was called the Su Wang Fu, simply referred to as the Fu, and held several thousand people, over five hundred of whom were children. Soldiers from the Japanese Legation were sent to defend the Fu while the remaining soldiers guarded the Legations. Throughout the siege, the Fu became the target of the heaviest artillery fire. The Chinese housed there were given white arm bands to wear, printed with the word "Christian," so they would not be mistaken for hostile Chinese. Some of the Protestant missionaries also refused to leave their congregations and their numbers were absorbed by the Legations.

The diplomats and missionaries quickly organized committees for the day-to-day operations and defence of the Legations. There were committees to handle: food acquisition and distribution; defence—making sand bags, erecting barricades, fortifying buildings and walls, and establishing a fire-fighting brigade; logistics—registering and documenting the movements and quarters of everyone in the Legations; sanitation; and medical. A small hospital was even set up, manned by medical doctors from amongst the foreigners and missionaries. Everyone was assigned a responsibility, although the converts were given the most menial of tasks.

With over 3,000 people to feed, food in the Legations fast became a priority. Within the perimeter were a number of foreign and Chinese shops and warehouses from which they gleaned a large quantity of wheat, rice, corn, pulse, and sorghum. They also found great quantities of wine, but these were quickly drunk. On the Legations' grounds were a number of mules and ponies that had been used for racing events outside Peking but were now a source of meat. There was also a cow. When the cow was killed,

> an attaché of the British Legation sent for a part of (its) kidney as a great luxury, but it had been already distributed. The sympathetic superintendent of the meat apportionment, however, not wishing to disappoint him, sent the man the kidney of a horse "without note or comment"; afterwards meeting him, he inquired how he liked it. He had enjoyed it greatly, and remarked that while eating it he had forgotten that he was in China![100]

The Chinese converts fared less well in the food department. Besides being provided with the leftover entrails and heads of ponies and mules, as well as two ponies with phthisis, dogs, cats, magpies, crows, and sparrows were shot for their consumption.

Drinking water was supplied from eight wells in the British Legation. It was potable and did not have to be boiled. Heat for the buildings was provided by hundreds of thousands of pounds of coal, which was found in a warehouse. Demolished buildings afforded them all the kindling they needed, as well as abundant timber for fortifications.

All the shops in Peking that dealt in foreign goods, as well as a number of Chinese dwellings, were within the defence perimeter surrounding the Legations. From these they obtained a large amount of fabric, clothing, bedding, and miscellaneous supplies. The clothing and bedding were provided to the Chinese converts and anyone else who had arrived at the Legations with only the clothes on their back.

Another major priority, besides feeding and clothing the residents, was making sandbags for their defence. Day in and day out the demand was incessant. At first, Legation curtains and tablecloths were used. When that material ran out, any available fabric was appropriated, even the silks, satins, and brocades from the foreign stores. All foreign women and many Chinese women sewed all day, churning out thousands of ready sandbags that were then filled with dirt.

> One might see people of every nationality hard at the unaccustomed and fatiguing work—a long-robed priest of the Greek Church shoveling

---

[100] *China in Convulsion*, p. 424.

earth into a bag held by a wife of a (diplomat), the string tied by a little Chinese boy, and the bag carried off by the . . . Chaplain of the Legation.[101]

In total, the siege lasted eight weeks, from June 20th to August 14th, with the Legations successfully defended against the Imperial troops and Boxers who made massive attempts to dislodge and kill those within. The Chinese used rifles, canons, and explosives, tried to set fire to the Legations, and even dug underneath to plant mines. Meanwhile the Legations only had rifles and one cannon. On August 14, 1900, the Allied troops arrived. Of the more than nine hundred foreigners in Peking, including diplomats and their families, troops of eight nations, and missionaries, only fifty-six were killed and some 150 wounded. No record was kept of the Chinese casualties.

One of the saddest notes, however, though certainly a testament to mankind's overall depravity (as a general phenomenon and not specific to any one race or culture), were the atrocities committed by the Allied troops when relieving the Legations. On their march to Peking, various cities and villages such as T'ung Chou were looted and burned, and the women raped and disembowelled. These helpless and inoffensive villagers were slaughtered by the thousands and thrown into the Amur River until it was choked by bodies. For sport, the soldiers shot everyone in sight that resembled a "heathen" Chinese. Many of the Chinese who survived the carnage later died of cold and starvation as, thanks to the marauding troops, they no longer had homes and were unable to tend to or harvest their crops. These atrocities were long remembered and continued the ill will held toward foreigners.

Although the Foreign Powers and Roman Catholic Church sought indemnities for the lives lost and property destroyed in the Boxer uprising, Hudson Taylor of the CIM and some of the other Protestant societies did not believe that compensation should be sought. They did, however, make several requests: that the losses of the Chinese converts be compensated; that widows and orphans be provided for; that the province of Shansi, where most of the devastation took place, pay 500,000 taels, 1/10 to be paid each year for building schools and educating the people; that equal treatment be given to both converts and non-converts; and that lists of rioters be kept for punishment should they offend again.

---

[101] Ibid., p. 290.

Appendix G

John and Betty Stam

Afraid? Of What?
To feel the spirit's glad release?
To pass from pain to perfect peace,
The strife and strain of life to cease?
Afraid-of that?

Afraid? Of What?
Afraid to see the Saviour's face,
To hear His welcome, and to trace
From glory gleam from wounds of grace?
Afraid-of that?

Afraid? Of What?
A flash, a crash, a pierced heart;
Darkness, light, O Heaven's art!
A wound of His a counterpart!
Afraid-of that?

Afraid? Of what?
To do by death what life could not—
Baptize with blood a stony plot,
Till souls shall blossom from the spot?
Afraid-of that?

December 6, 1934 was a bleak, wintery day in Tsingteh, a small brick-walled town in South Anhwei. It was a secluded town, hidden like a jewel in the heart of rugged natural beauty. Set on a hill, it was only accessible to the outside world by stone paths that cut through the mountains. American CIM missionaries John and Betty Stam and their three-month-old daughter, Helen Priscilla, lived there in a rented shop front that served not only as their home but a preaching chapel as well. It was the Stams' first posting of their own after John finished language school at Hwaining.

That morning, various townspeople appeared at their door, warning them that Communist forces were near and urging them to flee. "Do you think we should leave, John?" asked Betty as she bathed little Helen, never realizing it would be the last time she would do so. "We'll wait and see," replied John.

As the Stams waited, the Communists piled into the town, having crossed the mountains by unfrequented paths and bypassing the Nationalist forces sixty miles to the south. Gunshots sounded in the streets as the looting began. By this time it was too late for John and Betty to flee even if they had wanted to. Better stay and weather the storm, they decided. A faithful cook and maid at the mission station stayed with them, and the Stams knelt with them in prayer. Then: pounding at the front gate. Communist soldiers broke the lock and marched into the courtyard. John spoke courteously to them, asking if they were hungry, and brought them into the family's living quarters. Betty served them tea and cakes. The courtesy meant nothing. The soldiers demanded all of their money, which John handed over. Then the soldiers bound John as he pleaded for the safety of his family. Leaving Betty and the baby behind, John was taken to the make-shift Communist headquarters.

The soldiers reappeared a short time later, demanding that Betty and the baby accompany them. The maid and cook pleaded to go, too, but were deterred when the soldiers threatened to shoot them. "It is better for you to stay here," Betty whispered. "If anything happens to us, look after the baby."

Like John, Betty was bound and placed in the local prison. In order to make room for them, some of the local prisoners were released. In the midst of the chaos, Helen started to cry, and a soldier suggested, in front of the hapless parents, that they kill her since she was only in their way. Then one of the prisoners who had just been released asked why they should kill the innocent baby. "Why kill her? What harm has she done?" he asked. "Are you a Christian?" demanded one of the guards. The man said he was not; he was one of the prisoners just released. "Then it's your life for hers," said the guard. The man was summarily executed as Betty hugged Helen to her chest.

The small family was held for ransom, and John was instructed to write a letter to CIM authorities in Shanghai asking for money. The letter was never delivered, but was later found bundled up in some of Helen's clothes. It read:

Dear Brethern,

My wife, baby and myself are today in the hands of Communists in the city of Tsingteh. Their demand is twenty thousand dollars for our release.

All our possessions and stores are in their hands, but we praise God for peace in our hearts and a meal tonight. God grant you wisdom in what you do, and us fortitude, courage and peace of heart. He is able—and a wonderful friend in such a time.

Things happened so quickly this a.m. They were in the city just a few hours after the ever-persistent rumors really became alarming, so that we could not prepare to leave in time. We were just too late.

The Lord bless and guide you, and as for us, may God be glorified whether by life or death.[102]

In Him,
John C. Stam[103]

The next morning, the Stams were forced to march twelve miles west through the mountains to the small town of Miao Sheo. John carried little Helen, but Betty, who was not physically strong owing to a youthful bout with inflammatory rheumatism, was allowed to ride a horse part of the way.

That night the Stams were held in the former house of a wealthy man, which was being used as a prison. Soldiers guarded them. John was tied to a post for the entire cold night, unable to move or even change his position, but Betty was allowed enough movement to tend to the baby.

Sometime during the night or in the wee hours of the morning, when not being watched by the soldiers, Betty dressed the baby in a little gown that she had made especially for her, put her in a hooded bunting bag, and hid her in a pile of heavy winter bedding. A change of clothes and some diapers were tucked into the sleeping bag, and pinned between the articles of clothing were two five-dollar bills.

In the morning, John and Betty were stripped of their outer clothing and, dressed only in their undergarments, paraded down the streets of Miao Sheo. In their rush, the soldiers forgot about little Helen.

The couple's hands were tightly bound behind their backs. John walked barefoot, having given his socks to Betty. The soldiers jeered and called the local residents to come and see the execution. Onlookers lined both sides of the street as the Stams were led toward a small hill outside the town.

---

[102] Philippians 1:20.
[103] *The Triumph of John and Bettty Stam*, p. 130.

On the way to the execution, a Chinese pharmacist named Chang stepped out of the crowd and pleaded for the lives of the two foreigners. The soldiers ordered the man back into the crowd but he would not step back. Some of the soldiers then went to his house where they found a Chinese copy of the Bible and a book of hymns. The man was then led alongside the Stams to be executed with them for being a Christian. John pleaded for the man's life, but to no avail.

Outside of town on Eagle Hill, in a clump of pine trees, the Stams were briefly allowed to stand together and were able to exchange a few words with each other. John was then ordered to kneel and, as he was quietly praying, a soldier swung his sword through John's throat. Betty did not scream. She quivered slightly and, bound as she was, fell on her knees beside John. Kneeling there, the same sword ended her life with a single blow, nearly severing her head from her body.

The date was December 8, 1934. John Stam was only twenty-seven years old. Betty was twenty-eight.

Nearby in the mountains was a group of refuges in hiding from Communist forces. For two days and two nights they suffered cold and hunger in their mountain refuge. Among them was a Chinese evangelist named Pastor Lo Ke-Chou. Through informants, he learned that the Communists had captured two foreigners. At first he did not realize that these were John and Betty Stam, with whom he had worked, but as he received more details he put two and two together. As soon as government troops arrived in the vicinity and it was safe to venture forth, Pastor Lo hurried into town. His questions were met with silence—everyone was fearful that spies might report anyone who said too much.

An old woman whispered to Pastor Lo that a baby had been left behind. She nodded in the direction of the house where John and Betty had been chained on their last night on Earth. Pastor Lo hurried to the site and found room after room that had been trashed by the soldiers. Then he heard a muffled cry. Tucked away by her mother in the little bunting bag, Helen was warm and alive, although hungry and thirsty after her two-day ordeal. Why did the baby not cry and alert the soldiers to her presence when they were trashing the room? How did she survive? In the bunting bag Pastor Lo found the money, miraculously still where it had been placed in faith and love by a tender mother, doubtless that it might save her little one's life.

The kindly pastor took the child in his arms and carried her to his wife. Then he went to attend to the bodies of John and Betty. After obtaining two coffins, he carefully sewed the gashes on their necks so they would look more natural, wrapped them in white cotton cloth, and sealed them in the coffins. He explained to the gathered crowd that the missionaries had only come to tell them how they might find forgiveness in Christ. Although the crowd dispersed thereafter, the coffins remained on the grassy hillside for another forty days before government help was secured to bring them out for burial.

Pastor Lo was now anxious to get Helen to safety. He was also worried about his own child, a little boy of four, who was desperately ill from cold and exposure. Pastor Lo had to find a way to carry the children a hundred miles through mountains infested with Communists and bandits. Brave men were found who were willing to help bear the children to safety and, with the money left by Betty, they now had the funds for travel. Hiding the children in large rice baskets slung from two ends of a bamboo carrying pole, the group departed quietly, taking turns carrying the precious cargo over their shoulders. Mrs. Lo was able to find Chinese mothers along the way to nurse Helen and, at one place, Lactogen—milk powder of a special brand, a rare commodity in those parts. Mrs. Lo was one of the few people who knew the proper formula, having previously worked in a mission hospital and taught the foreign way of caring for infants. She even had on hand the feeding bottle used for her own baby, and was able to put little Helen on a proper three-hour feeding schedule. On foot, the group made it safely through the perils, and Lo's own boy recovered fully.

Six days later, a missionary in Suanchen heard a rap at his door. He opened it and a Chinese woman, stained with travel, entered the house, bearing a bundle in her arms. "This is all we have left," she said brokenly.

The missionary took the bundle and turned back the blanket to uncover the sleeping face of Helen Priscilla Stam. Many kind hands had laboured to preserve the infant girl, but none kinder than Betty, who had spared no effort for her baby even as she faced degradation and death.

Helen Priscilla was examined by a doctor at the mission hospital and pronounced in perfect health. From there she was placed in the care of Betty's parents, Dr. Charles Scott and Mrs. Clara Scott, who were also missionaries in China.

Many days later, when it was safe to do so, John and Betty's coffins were brought from Maio Sheo for a post-mortem medical examination. At the missionary hospital in Wuhu, the heavy coffin lids were lifted to reveal the bodies, lying on their backs, modestly clothed in their underwear—just as they had been forced to walk the streets of Maio Sheo a month and a half earlier. Each casket contained probably one hundred pounds of lime. The bodies, wrapped in clean, white cotton sheeting were preserved and in good condition. Apart from deep rope burns on John's wrists, there was no evidence of mutilation or abuse.

John's straight, aquiline nose and jutting chin were tilted in his customary posture of candour and open friendliness. His lips were parted in an expectant smile. One could easily believe that when the sword struck, tearing a savage hole in the front of his throat, he saw beyond his assassin to the angel hosts at the portals of heaven. Certainly there was no sign of fear or terror, leading to the conclusion that the attack was sudden, death almost immediate. What great love by Pastor Lo to make an attempt to stitch up the torn throat to make it more respectable!

With Betty, it was somewhat different. On her face, serenity blended with terror and consternation. Obviously she'd witnessed what had happened to her husband. But at the same time a heavy sword swung across her neck from behind, almost severing her head from her body. Still, Pastor Lo had succeeded in sewing her head so that it appeared intact.

What struck the medical personnel who saw the bodies, what made the sight of them unforgettable, was the quiet peace and expectancy etched onto the faces of the two martyrs.

Today, the bodies lie buried in a little Christian cemetery on a quiet hillside in the city of Wuhu. There they wait an Easter deliverance that was denied them on Earth. The handful of China Inland missionaries and local Christians who were there at the simple burial service took comfort in God's assurance: "My ways are not your ways; neither are your ways My ways."

The Stams' gravestones read:

John Cornelius Stam, January 18, 1907, "That Christ may be glorified whether by life or by death." Philippians 1:20

Elisabeth Scott Stam, February 22, 1906, "For me to live is Christ and to die is gain." Philippians 1:21

Florence: A Missionary in China

December 8, 1934, Miao Sheo, Anhui, "Be though faithful unto death and I will give thee a crown of life." Revelation 2:10

As for the Communists responsible for the Stams' deaths, they met their end shortly thereafter. After killing the Stams, they joined up with the Red 10th Army, which was annihilated in its entirety by Nationalist forces on January 27, 1935.[104]

---

[104] The preceding is a composite account of the martyrdom of John and Betty Stam taken from various sources, including Geraldine Taylor's *The Triumph of John and Betty Stam*; John and Betty Stam Martyred 1901–2000 Church History Timeline; John and Betty Stam—GFA Missions; For the Stams No Deliverance, East Asia's Millions, November/December 1984; and Murder of John and Betty Stam, Wikipedia.

Bibliography

Andrews, Marion. *My China Mystery*. Australia: Even Before Publishing, 2012.

Austin, Alvyn J. *Saving China*. Toronto: University of Toronto Press, 1986.

Bosshardt, Alfred. *The Guiding Hand*. London: Hodder and Stoughton, 1973.

Brady, Anne-Marie. *A Foreign Missionary on the Long March: The Unpublished Memoirs of Arnolis Hayman of the China Inland Mission*. Portland, Maine: Merwinasia, 2011.

Brackman, Arnold C. *The Other Nuremberg: The Untold Story of the Tokyo War Crimes Trials*. New York: Quill, 1987.

Brandt, Nat. *Massacre in Shansi*. U.S.A.: Syracuse University Press, 1994.

Broomhall, Marshall. *Martyred Missionaries of the China Inland Mission*. London: Morgan & Scott, 1901.

Buck, Pearl S. *My Several Worlds*. New York: Pocket Books, 1954.

Chang, Iris. *The Rape of Nanking*. U.S.A.: Basic Books, 1997.

Chennault, Claire Lee. *Way of a Fighter*. New York: G. P. Putnam's Sons, 1949.

Clements, Ronald and Metcalf, Steve. *In Japan the Crickets Cry*. Oxford: Monarch Books, 2010.

Cliff, Norman. *Courtyard of the Happy Way*. England: Arthur James Limited, 1977.

Cliff, Norman (Ed.). *How Firm a Foundation*. Chefoo Schools Association, 2006.

Crossett, Margaret. *Harvest at the Front*. U.S.A.: China Inland Mission, 1946.

De Jaegher, Raymond J. and Kuhn, Irene Corbally. *The Enemy Within*. Bandra, Bombay: St. Paul Publications, 1969.

Doolittle, Gardner. *Wings of a Warrior*. DVD, Shelter Island, 2013.

Doolittle, James. *I Could Never Be So Lucky Again*. New York: Bantam Books, 1991.

Dunn, Miriam. *My Children or the Cross*. Dalton, Ohio: P. Graham Dunn Publishing, 2011.

Ferguson, Carol. *God's Mimic: The Biography of Hazel Page*. Victoria, B.C.: Trafford Publishing, 2005.

Fischer, Louis. *Gandhi*. New York: New American Library, 1954.

Gardella, Robert (Ed.). *Missions to China's Heartland, The Letters of Hazel Todd of the China Inland Mission, 1920–1941*. Portland, Maine: Merwinasia, 2009.

Gilkey, Langdon. *Shantung Compound*. New York: Harper & Row, 1966.

Glines, Carroll V. *Doolittle's Tokyo Raiders*. New York: D. Van Nostrand Company, Inc., 1964.

Glines, Carroll V. *Four Came Home*. New York: D. Van Nostrand Company, Inc., 1966.

Goldstein, Norm (Ed.). *China From the Long March to Tiananmen Square*. New York: Henry Holt and Company, 1990.

Greenough, Jan. *Courage in Dark Places*. London: Monarch Books, 2002.

Greenough, Jan. *Faith in Tough Places*. London: Monarch Books, 2002.

Hahn, Emily. *Chiang Kai-Shek*. New York: Doubleday & Company, 1955.

Hefley, James and Marti. *The Secret File on John Birch*. Hannibal Books, 1995.

Hu, Hua-ling. *American Goddess at the Rape of Nanking: The Courage of Minnie Vautrin*. Carbondale and Edwardsville: Southern Illinois University Press, 2000.

Lawless, A. C. *Under His Wings*. Philippines: Action International, 2003.

Lawson, Ted. *Thirty Seconds Over Tokyo*. New York: Pocket Star Books, 2002.

Locke, George H. (Ed.). *The World Book*. Toronto: W. W. Quarrie & Company, 1923, pp. 5336–5337.

Magnusson, Sally. *The Flying Scotsman*. London: Quartet Books, 1981.

Martinson, Harold M. *Red Dragon Over China*. Minneapolis: Augsburg Publishing House, 1956.

McRoberts, Duncan. *Pleading China*. Grand Rapids, Michigan: Zondervan Publishing House, 1946.

McRoberts, Duncan. *While China Bleeds*. Grand Rapids, Michigan: Zondervan Publishing House, 1943.

Michell, David. *A Boy's War*. U.S.A.: Overseas Missionary Fellowship, 1988.

Miller, Sheila. *Pigtails, Petticoats and the Old School Tie*. Belmont: OMF, 1981.

Overseas Missionary Fellowship. *God's Faithfulness*. OMF International, 2014.

Pakula, Hannah. *The Last Empress*. New York: Simon & Schuster, 2009.

Paulson, Philip. *Captured!, Young Pilot, March and April, 1965*. Three Hills, Alberta: PBI, pp. 24, 30–31; pp. 29–31.

Payne, Robert. *The Life and Death of Mahatma Gandhi*. New York: Konecky & Konecky, 1969.

Phillips, Clifford H. *The Lady Named Thunder*. Edmonton, Alberta: University of Alberta Press, 2003.

Pu Yi, Aisin Gioro (Henry). *From Emperor to Citizen*. Oxford: Oxford University Press, 1987.

Rabe, John. *The Good Man of Nanking*. New York: Vintage Books, 1998.

Roberts, Neel. *No Solitary Effort*. Pasadena, Calif.: William Carey Library, 2013.

Scott, Munroe. *McClure, The China Years*. New York: Penguin Books, 1977.

Seagrave, Sterling. The *Soong Dynasty*. New York: Harper & Row, 1985.

Smedley, Agnes. *Battle Hymn of China*. London: Victor Gollancz, Ltd., 1944.

Smith, Arthur. *China in Convulsion, Volumes One and Two*. London: Forgotten Books, 2017.

Snow, Edgar. *Red Star Over China.* New York: Bantam Books, 1978.

Suyin, Han. *The Morning Deluge: Mao Tsetung & the Chinese Revolution, 1893–1954.* Boston: Little, Brown & Company, 1972.

Taylor, Geraldine. *The Triumph of John and Betty Stam.* U.S.A.: OMF Books, 2012.

Taylor, Jay. *The Generalissimo.* Cambridge, Massachusetts: Harvard University Press, 2009.

Thiessen, Evangeline. *With Sails on His Bike.* Belleville, Ontario: Guardian Books, 2008.

Thompson, Phyllis. *China: The Reluctant Exodus.* U.S.A.: OMF Books, 2000.

Thompson, R. E. and Ella. *Missionary Discipleship.* U.S.A.: Missionary Internship, 1982.

Thomson, H. C. *The Case for China.* London: C. Tinling & Co., Ltd., 1933.

Tipton, Laurance. *Chinese Escapade.* London: MacMillan & Co., 1949.

Vautrin, Minnie. *Terror in Minnie Vautrin's Nanjing.* Chicago: University of Illinois Press, 2008.

Watson, Charles Hoyt. *De Shazer.* Winona Lake, Indiana: The Light and Life Press, 1950.

Watson, Jean. *Bosshardt: A Biography.* Great Britain: Monarch Publications, 1988.

Weatherby, W. J. *Chariots of Fire.* New York: Dell/Quicksilver, 1981.

White, Theodore H. *China: The Roots of Madness.* New York: W. W. Norton & Company Inc., 1968.

Williamson, Glen. *Geneva.* U.S.A.: The Light and Life Press, 1974.

About the Author

Marguerite Joy Paulson is the youngest of seven children born to Florence and Clifford Paulson. She was given her second name, Joy, by her father who said that the word Joy in the Bible had a special meaning for him because of her.

In 1972 Marguerite obtained a Bachelor of Arts degree in Sociology, and then travelled in Europe and Africa for a year, where she gained immeasurable life experience. Later, she obtained a Masters of Science and a Doctoral degree from the University of Calgary. In 1987 she had the pleasure of accompanying her mother on a return trip to China.

In her professional life Marguerite has worked as a clinical and forensic psychologist, and is currently in private practice in a small rural community in northern Alberta.

She is thankful for being raised in a Christian home by God-fearing parents and for the example they provided of a life of integrity and love of others, in particular the Chinese people, and their faithfulness to God's calling. In the Bible it says, "Yea, a man may say, Thou hast faith, and I have works: shew me thy faith without thy works, and I will shew thee my faith by my works" (James 2:18). My parents certainly expressed their faith by their actions and life.

Email:mjpaulson@abnorth.com

Acknowledgements

I would like to thank the following people whose assistance enabled me to fulfill my desire to write my mother's story:

Natalie Johnson, my sister Lucille Gishler, and my brother Duane Paulson for their editorial suggestions, as well as Duane's review and written documentation of the fight between the little grey mongoose and king cobra.

My friend, L. P. Suzanne Atkinson, a well-published author, who shared her knowledge and encouraged me to see that my endeavours might have some merit.

Andrew Wilmot for the copy-editing.

Donna Antkowiak for the cover design and layout of the manuscript.

My two good friends and primary sources of support—Harriet Sawatzky for typing the manuscript and Barb Monita for her tireless computer searches; both for their undying patience.

All Scripture quotations are from the *King James Version of the Bible*, unless otherwise indicated.

Florence's letters have been replicated as written, without alteration.

Historical place names have been retained and are romanised in form.

Newspaper articles have been reproduced from the original.

Maps are not drawn to scale. They are included to reference locations where Florence served or travelled.

www.ingramcontent.com/pod-product-compliance
Lightning Source LLC
Chambersburg PA
CBHW071236070526
44583CB00017B/2207